MW00791284

"Sally Klein O'Connor takes us on a redemptive journey into darkness and it's there we see the light of God's great love. The camps of the Holocaust are perhaps the darkest places on earth. But in obedience to God, Sally and her team decided to reach out to people, Jew and Gentile, with the light of the love of Jesus by simply handing out beautiful red roses. Through these small steps, the Spirit of God brings illumination. The light He shines reveals not only the evils of the Nazis, but the darkness of resentment, shame and bitterness that reside in every human heart.

The story reminds us that a most common human response to suffering is denial; just bury it and move on. This book is about grace, forgiveness, and reconciliation, but offers no easy answers. Filled with testimonies of what Jesus can do if His people will simply go first, this book will make you think deeply about taking the first steps of forgiveness and reconciliation."

Bill Dwyer
Senior Pastor
Valley Vineyard Christian Fellowship
Reseda, California

"Few books illustrate God's grace in action as powerfully as Sally Klein O'Connor's *A Rumor of Roses*. The remarkable accounts of her rose-in-hand outreaches to the descendants of those who showed The Jewish people the least mercy teach us a lesson in unconditional love that both challenges and inspires us. You will ponder the extraordinary message of *A Rumor of Roses* long after you finish reading it."

Michael Robert Wolf
Author, The Linotype Operator and
The Other: The Linotype Legacy

"Sally Klein O'Connor's *A Rumor of Roses* will both bless and anger, comfort and confront anyone who reads it. Her book is a powerful and indispensable reminder of the Gospel truth that Jesus didn't die for us because we were His friends. He died for us while we were His enemies. At the same time, it is a penetrating challenge to love our neighbors as we love ourselves, including those who hate us or those whom we currently hate. We're left standing with a question to ourselves that most of us would rather not ask. 'Just how real is the Gospel to me?' Whether you agree or disagree with what Sally writes, *A Rumor of Roses* is a critical book that will cause you to wrestle and grow."

Avi Snyder
European Director
Jews for Jesus

"In *A Rumor of Roses*, Sally unpacks challenges that could have caused her to retreat to a safe zone and allow the world to go wherever it's going, but she chose rather to reach out to humanity with the love of her Savior.

One of the very practical and novel ways Sally has reached out to humanity has been the organizing of several 'Tour of Roses,' where she and team members hand out roses to people they meet on city streets across the world. This is such a unique way to connect with people and communicate to them how much God loves them. The roses speak of beauty, the beauty of the people. But they also speak of the blood of Jesus, shed for the forgiveness of sin, and also of love— the love of God, a love that Sally has shared across the world, including Northern Ireland, Poland, Germany and Israel, and now also here, in this book *A Rumor of Roses*.

Jack McKee MBE
Senior Pastor
New Life City Church
Belfast, Northern Ireland

"Having had A Tour of Roses in our community, I very much enjoyed reading Sally and her team's experiences. Of the thousands of roses given away throughout the years, it will be very interesting to see the part they have played in God's Grand Plan of Redemption. A very compelling account of what can happen when one dares to trust the Lord in the hearing and obeying his quiet voice."

Frank Kowal
Senior Pastor
Jubilee Church
Kenora, Ontario, Canada

"*A Rumor of Roses* is a unique book the same way A Tour of Roses is a unique ministry. This book took me back to the days of A Tour of Roses in Łódź (2014) and I started to read carefully, day by day, using it in the same way as a devotional lecture. I think this book is so important for us—the Polish people as a nation—because of our national history. It is so important for me—and for us as human beings—because of our sometimes very painful personal stories… God's love is always the answer. When Sally came to Łódź I needed A Tour of Roses. Now I receive *A Rumor of Roses* as a strong encouragement and message. Even now, as I read, I find some of God's medicine for me in it. I strongly recommend this book."

Piotr M. Karas
Senior Pastor
New Life Pentecostal Church
Łódź, Poland

"*A Rumor of Roses* is a very important book. Its passages about forgiveness of those who have wronged us are profound and necessary for anyone seeking a closer, sincere walk with God."

Rabbi Dr. Michael Schiffman

"Upon reading *A Rumor of Roses*, it touched my heart deeply. Our congregation is no stranger to reconciliation and forgiveness, as we actively participate in an annual event of fellowship between Messianic Jews and Arab Christians. Sally presents a challenge to us all. 'How much forgiving of one another is enough?' And it all begins with reading this book that is written from her heart."

Rabbi Corey Sylvester
Temple Aviv Judea
Fullerton, California

a RUMOR of ROSES

a RUMOR of ROSES

Planting Seeds of God's Extravagant Love

By
Sally Klein O'Connor

IPM Books
North Hollywood, California

Printed in the United States of America
Print ISBN-978-1-7334643-0-7
eBook ISBN-978-1-7334643-1-4

Published by IPM Books, an imprint of
Improbable People Ministries
North Hollywood, California
USA

Unless otherwise noted, Scripture quotations are from the Holy Bible,
New International Version, copyright © 1973, 1978, 1984 by
International Bible Society and New King James Version.

Cover Design & Layout
Nadine Erickson
nadinespage@gmail.com

Interior Design & Layout
Tracy Atkins
TheBookMakers.com

Professional Editing
Carol Lerner
clerner44@gmail.com

Dedicated to my Dad,
Dave Klein, who worked with flowers for over 50 years.

CONTENTS

AUTHOR'S NOTE

A bit of business before we engage:

Some of the names used in this narrative are aliases so that people who live in compromising situations will not be threatened.

My use of italics will generally be restricted to the introductory quotes for each chapter, impressions of God speaking to me, words or phrases that need emphasis, some journal entries, and book titles.

The term "believers" will generally refer to people who have been born again in Yeshua/Jesus the Messiah, and are committed to walking in His way.

Lastly, some of the dialogue is reconstructed from reports and notes, and less-than-perfect memory. The essence is intact.

INTRODUCTION

A friend asked me the very first time we prepared to bring several hundred roses to some of the more infamous towns of WWII in Germany and Poland, "Do you think everything God has brought you through in your life has been to prepare you for this moment—this vision?"

My dad was a florist for 50 years. All during my childhood he owned and managed what became a well-known shop (at least among florists in the know) on Hollywood and Vermont in Los Angeles. My mom came up with the name—Dave's Flowerland. Last time I checked the shop still stands.

Buds and blooms may be fragile and very beautiful, but the business can be tough. Getting up around 1 or 2AM to catch his favorite growers down at the Wholesale Market in the heart of Downtown Los Angeles was no small thing. My father worked long days.

The shop was open 7 days a week, on any and all holidays. Our lives revolved around the business, though my brother and I were too small to notice at first.

Six days a week Dad came home late smelling like carnations, sweat, and stale cigarettes. When I was still small I would run to the door and greet him. He would briefly acknowledge my hug, then head for a long hot bath and the paper.

As I got older I spent most of the holidays working at the shop. Mom was the main designer, overseeing some others who learned from her. My brother and I were allowed to roam freely as long as we didn't get in the way of a sale or of the designers working on arrangements. I think my first job, besides sweeping up, was folding boxes. I stayed in the back for hours at a time, folding many different kinds of boxes for corsages, for roses, and to hold many types of flower arrangements. No one else wanted to do it so Dad was glad for my help. Later, when I was a little older, I learned how to clean and prepare roses.

Dad demonstrated by taking a pair of strippers (also known as scratchers), closing them together over the stem about halfway up its length and firmly pulling it down the stem. It tore off thorns and leaves all in one swift movement, leaving the rose naked halfway down, making it much easier to handle. When I became fairly proficient in handling the strippers, I learned how to "petal." This required some discernment. It consisted of plucking off bad petals—torn, dirty, or odd-looking ones from the head of the rose—so it appeared younger and fresher. More perfect.

Cleaning roses was a job without end. Bunches and bunches of different colors, kinds, and sizes of roses, all rubberbanded with their heads carefully wrapped in paper and stapled so they wouldn't snap off their stems in transit from grower to market to flower shop. I ran through a lot of bandaids in those early years of cleaning and petaling roses

Sometime just before my teens, Dad began inviting me to accompany him occasionally to the Wholesale Flower Market. I'd get up in the middle of the night, while everything was still dark and mostly quiet—even in L.A.—climb up into his truck, and power along the almost empty Hollywood Freeway toward Downtown and the wholesale flower district. In those days many Asians ran the market and my father had a nickname among them—"Hollywood Dave." He would poke and prod to get the very best price and sometimes when I looked back at the faces of his "friends" they were not so happy. But Dad was thrilled. Small victories made his day.

Afterward we would sit at breakfast, in the smoke-filled greasy spoon where everyone in the business hung out, and Dad would order his little slice of heaven—eggs and bacon or ham. Dad was Jewish, raised orthodox, and for whatever reason, though we didn't keep kosher, bacon/ham/pig in general never crossed the threshold of our house. But Dad would sneak off to get his taste of *treif* (any food that is considered non-kosher, like pig or shellfish, etc.) down at the market—

or sometimes at Norm's, a little closer to home—and then he would return to the shop with all his hard-won wholesale treasures. Unpacking, cutting stems, and bucketing all the flowers in water ensued, usually followed by cleaning the roses.

My dad and I didn't have much of a relationship in those days. Fishing and flowers were the perilously thin threads tying us together. I accumulated a lot of anger toward him because of choices he made as our father. But looking back I don't think my father was malicious. His relational tools were limited as was his ability to process the growing problems in our family, and the frustration of our situation often got the best of him.

I never wanted to be in the flower business when I grew up. I wanted to sing, write, and act—anything but flowers. But flowers were what I knew, and it opened doors of employment for me. During my college years I worked in shops in Boston, Manhattan, and eventually back in Los Angeles.

Because my father was unable to entirely retire gracefully, every now and then—on Valentine's or Mother's Day—he would stake out a corner somewhere in the valley and sniff around the wholesale market downtown to see what he could scrounge up in the way of a deal. After my initial homecoming from college, Dad would periodically invite me to participate in his holiday guerrilla tactics. He never had a permit, but we would set up a little stand on a corner with lots of outrageous signs and start selling. The signs were always about how cheap the roses were. We usually made some good money, but it was always hard to work with Dad.

I was 9 months pregnant the last time I ever stood out on a corner with Dad selling flowers. The police came and demanded to see his license to sell. Dad fussed and fumbled as if there actually was a proper piece of paper somewhere in his possession, all the while gesturing to me to keep selling to as many customers as possible. Eventually, the police shut us down for the day, but not before they threatened to take us to jail. After that episode I lost my taste for dealing flowers on street corners—until more recently.

It's funny how God uses everything in our lives. There is no waste in the Kingdom of God. He is a Redeemer, even of things we would rather forget.

—Sally Klein O'Connor

1

KADOSH

K*adosh.*

Just the whisper of His voice shivered my soul. The wind curled the last of it away over the tops of what remained of the worn and beaten barracks of Birkenau. Here men and women sweated and stunk, slept and starved together, crying out to their Creator to deliver them.

How can *this* place—of all places—be kadosh? These grounds are incontrovertible evidence Evil exists. How can *this* place be holy?

Kadosh.

I heard the rush of sound again, rustling the last autumn leaves on the slim trees near the ruins of the crematoriums. But as I looked into the thick water of the little pools nearby, all I could think was, *"Ashes, ashes, we all fall down..."*

Inside the exhibit there were names and faces, pictures from some other era when people who were marched into this place had laughed, sung and loved together, married and raised families. Hope was not yet a four-letter word, but a natural fruit of faith—faith in the one true God.

I Am.

How can You be in this place?

I Am. I Was. And I will be.

I had not expected this. Tears, anger, fear—there were so many things I thought about as I planned this trip. But I never considered God was here.

It was October 2007, and on the grounds where I stood almost a million Jewish people had been exterminated. As I looked out through the gate, I noticed a group of houses staring back at me. Maybe two city blocks away, they sat on their cold foundations facing me without pity. I looked at them, amazed. Windows, curtains, and colors—how could anyone live so close to such a place as Birkenau? Why would anyone choose to raise a family next to a killing field?

My friend Evi Hall and I had seen Bergen-Belsen a couple of days before. It was wild and strangely beautiful. Little pink flowers spread their petals between large stone markers numbering the bodies buried there. I wrote in my journal:

The forest keeps its own secrets. How old are the trees? Did the blood of victims water some of their roots? The land gives no hint, no evidence, no witness. It grows and flourishes according to God's design regardless of human history. It is seemingly indifferent to what took place.

In Bergen-Belsen, as in Auschwitz-Birkenau, it seemed unjust that any life could flourish in the same soil which received the blood of so many. Places like these should be sentenced to barrenness forever. The very soil rendered incapable of giving the least nourishment for even the basest life. Why should anything green grow in any place where innocence was murdered? It was almost as if the evidence of what happened might be swallowed up in the remorseless flowers and trees that flourished in such places. As if it might be erased entirely if we weren't careful.

My heart railed against God: *Why doesn't this look like Sodom and Gomorrah? Why should there be any kind of beauty at all in a place like this?*

The answer came without apology.

I am a Redeemer, how about you?
I am about life. How about you?

Lord God,

We remember that You are the Creator God, the Maker of the Heavens and the Earth, and that You spoke into existence all that was and is—all that breathes and grows—from nothing at all. And this earth, where we stand, belongs to You. And Lord, You gave man the position of ruler and caretaker over the earth, but only You can redeem the earth from the foulness and stain of man's depravity and sin.

Lord, we recognize that the whole earth groans, longing for Your final redemption, as it says in Romans. But we stand here this day, Lord, where the blood of thousands stained the earth as the result of Cain's legacy, because brother turned against brother. We cry out for Your forgiveness and your healing, for the land and its people. For those who spoke the words that brought to pass these atrocities, for those whose hands committed the deeds, and for those who looked the other way while family and neighbors and friends were slaughtered and their blood stained the earth and their ashes choked the air.

O God, have mercy on all of us. We are all capable of such hatred in our hearts as long as sin rules in us. Lord, we cry out on behalf of those who were killed, and ask God for Your healing and mercy to cleanse, bind up, and redeem. To speak Your goodness into the hearts of their children and their children's children, and all their lineage from this place—and we commit them to Life!

Let them no longer be bound by the horror and the weight of these chains. And while they will never forget throughout the generations, let Your love cleanse and heal these deep wounds and lead them out from the chains of hatred into that vast and generous place where Your love and mercy follow them wherever they go. Where they are free to taste and see that the Lord is good.

And, Father, with one voice we cry out for Your mercy and forgiveness to be poured out from heaven upon the land and the people of this place. That the greatness of Your goodness would be seen once again by the people of this land and the chains of hatred and fear and shame and condemnation would be broken forever by the shed blood of Jesus Christ. Let Your blood cover the stain of blood in this place and restore the people and the land to the knowledge of Your great goodness, Your loving kindness, the abundant provision of Your grace. Let it bend us to our knees, bring our faces to the earth.

Who are we—any of us—that You are even mindful of us? Yet it is Your great love that bought us from the grave and from sin's mastery. Lord, this day in prayer, we add our voices to the many who have and are interceding, and we consecrate this place and this people to You, who are Life, that You would resurrect from the dead this land and its people so that they may walk in all Your ways, and most especially in the way of Love.

Amen.

"If only there were vile people... committing evil deeds, and it were only necessary to separate them from the rest of us and destroy them. But the line dividing good and evil cuts through the heart of every human being. And who is willing to destroy a piece of his own heart?... One and the same human being is, at various ages, under various circumstances, a totally different human being. At times he is close to being a devil, at times to sainthood. But his name doesn't change, and to that name we ascribe the whole lot, good and evil."

(from *The Gulag Archipelago*—Aleksandr Solzhenitsyn)

2

PERSPECTIVE

Sometime ago it became a habit of mine on Sunday nights to take off down Interstate 5 South to Lynwood and hang out at a friend's church. The Holy Spirit manifested there in some powerful ways and more often than not, the Lord would speak to my heart through the worship and teaching.

After one particular evening service at Lyn-Gate Neighborhood Church, my new friend, Debbie, began talking about her upcoming trip to Germany. She had recently ministered to some young German believers while they were stateside and they invited her to visit and minister at their home church.

Debbie, also a Jewish believer, surprised me by not showing any reluctance about visiting Germany. In fact, she seemed eager to experience whatever the Lord might do there. But she had a particular concern. In discussing plans with her young German hosts she broached the idea of visiting one of the former concentration camps during her upcoming stay. Their reaction was not what she anticipated. They were deeply offended. They responded very emotionally to the idea, asking her:

"When will this be over? How long is this going to go on?"

"This," as we both understood it to be, referred to the aftermath of the Holocaust and how the Jewish community remembers what happened. As she detailed this exchange, I was offended by their reaction. Who were they to be upset? If she wanted to see one of the sites where our people were murdered by their people, what right did they have to stand in her way? Who were they to say they were done remembering? After all, *they* were the perpetrators—the bad guys. *We* were the victims.

I laid hands on my friend to intercede in prayer, filled with a righteous sense of indignation. It had become very clear to me that she was walking into enemy territory. But as I proceeded to pray, questions popped into my mind that never occurred to me before. As I continued pouring out what I thought to be a totally justified petition on her behalf, a strong still whisper wove its way through my thoughts.

What do you think happened to the Germans after the war?

I had no idea. Why should I care? What they did was evil, inhuman. Besides, I am Jewish.

This was the fruit of all I knew and had been taught through family and culture. It was beyond any understanding I possessed how anyone could see the situation differently. I pressed on in prayer for my friend.

How do you think the Germans feel about what happened in the Holocaust?

The question startled me. No one I knew had ever expressed such ideas. It was always about what happened to the Jews and the need to never forget because it might happen again. In fact, we were convinced as a community that it would most certainly happen again, despite all efforts to the contrary. Furthermore, *we* were the wounded party, along with the Roma, homosexuals, disabled, Russians, and political dissidents—all people who didn't conform to the Aryan ideal—but especially the Jews. Never did I—or anyone I knew—ponder for a moment what, if anything, the Germans might feel about what happened in the Holocaust. It was irrelevant. It was simply not worth considering because human beings didn't do the things they did.

But in the days and months that followed, many other thoughts began to thread their way through my head and heart.

What about the Germans? What did they lose? The "Fatherland" lost its fathers, brothers, and sons. In the slaughter of others they murdered their own humanity and soaked their land and people—and much of Europe—with innocent blood. After the war justice came down like a mighty hammer, smashing the German psyche (for the second time) in the hope that nothing as monstrous as the Nazis would ever surface again. Germany suffered utter humiliation and shame, and was made to repent by the world. But were they sorry or just numb? Did they even understand what they had done or did history and civilization just move on, leaving them stuttering and stumbling in its wake?

"Godly sorrow brings repentance that leads to salvation and leaves no regret, but worldly sorrow brings death." (2 Corinthians 7:10)

Germany never had a chance to consider or grieve all that was lost in WWII. They were indicted, tried, pronounced guilty, and punished. Being a practical people intent on surviving, they buried their dead, put away the war machines, picked themselves up from the remains and immediately began to rebuild their cities and lives. It was all they knew how to do. But their hearts never healed.

Perspective is a crazy thing. I remember being just eight years old when my whole world shifted. We had recently moved to a brand-new neighborhood and were still settling in. One morning I walked down the block to take the bus to school and a man had his dog out. It was a German Shepherd. I loved animals; we had two mutts at home. I asked if I could pet his dog because Mom taught me to always to ask first if a dog was friendly and didn't bite. The man affirmed his dog was safe. I bent down to get closer, lifting my hand over his head as I prepared to pet him. Without sound or warning the dog ripped open the right side of my face.

In the emergency room the neighbor, Mr. Smith, informed us his canine had just received a series of hormone shots the day before. He also reluctantly admitted his dog had attained a certain reputation in the neighborhood, of which I had been unaware, being the new kid on the block. The dog had nipped at several kids, chasing them down the street, and had bitten down pretty hard on one kid's finger. Mr. Smith knew all about what had happened in the neighborhood with his pet, but had refused to accept his dog might really be a threat.

At that point in my life all I knew was that Mr. Smith was a liar. It was pretty black and white to me. It didn't matter that he was very sorry, or that his favorite pet was taken from him and put to sleep forever. I was the one who experienced hurt and would have to carry this mark on my face for the rest of my life.

Now, more than half a lifetime removed from that event, I see more clearly. Mr. Smith was not so much a liar as he was living in denial. He didn't want to believe his pet was dangerous because that meant his world would have to change. Unfortunately, his unwillingness to see the truth cost him his dog, and in the process completely altered my life, and probably his.

Denial is a coping tool we all use at different times in our lives when the cold hard reality of a situation becomes too much to engage or process. We set reality aside, ignore it, go on as if nothing happened because it is the change we fear most. Mr. Smith knew that if he admitted his dog was prone to bite, it would mean things might be different. He might even lose his dog. He chose to ignore what he knew and didn't engage reality. He chose denial.

It is thought that many people in the towns and villages near the concentration camps in Germany and throughout Europe knew what was happening, but only a few extraordinary people risked their lives to intervene in some fashion. It has also been argued there was no possible way anyone could not have known. Only God, who hears the secrets of each human heart, will ever know for sure.

I believe there were signs all along the way that their new leader was not all they hoped he might be. There was a current of evil and hatred in his words and ways, and choices made that were against the very heart of God.

It seems impossible to many of us how people who lived nearby could ignore the stench of burning flesh, smoke and ashes. Or turn a deaf ear or blind eye to trains carrying people across the countryside boxed in like cattle with barbed wire. Did they turn their heads away when German society began to whisper? When friends and neighbors disappeared?

Germany also began to prosper under Hitler after a long period of extreme poverty and shame. And the German people, like Mr. Smith, may have wanted desperately to believe all was well—or mostly well. So they may have swerved aside from all the signs of the times and tuned their ears away from what they didn't want to hear. Hope and fear intermingled as war came upon them. And denial, for as long as they could, was a way of keeping drastic change at bay. How else could the people of the beautiful Bavarian town of Dachau have been so totally shocked by what they saw when the Allies marched them into the concentration camp to see the remains of the Nazi's handiwork?

The human ability to deny, compartmentalize, and rationalize is not to be minimized or ignored. And the price of that kind of repudiation has cost Germany over several generations now, even as it has cost Abraham's race and the world.

We approached two girls (they looked to be around 16 years old) with young children who looked very weary. We went over to them to hand them roses. They were really shocked and wondered why we would be doing this. I said, "Look how beautiful it is. That is how beautiful you are to God." One girl said she was going to cry.

(Elaine Stover—A *Tour of Roses*, Belfast 2013)

I extended a rose to a woman who was walking down the street and I frightened her. I apologized. She asked what the rose was for. I told her it was a gift to let her know that God loves her, and she said, "Oh, my gosh. You don't even know. I've been walking around in despair all day long." She told me she needed to know something by Friday and she let me pray for her. After I prayed for her, she told me, "God sent you to me today." She asked me to please not forget her. Her name was Margaret.

(Kathy Bradshaw—A *Tour of Roses*, Belfast 2013)

3

DRIVING MISS BRENDA

The first time I ever traveled to The Emerald Isle was in 2004. My new friend, Donna Taggart, and her daughter, Jodie, arranged for me to do a concert at their gathering in Newtonards. It was a good crowd considering they only had three weeks' notice. I included some of our more humorous songs. I remember how some people remarked after the concert how good it was to laugh—they had never considered it acceptable to laugh in church.

Donna, good hostess that she is, asked if I wanted to see one of the tourist spots before taking the train back to Dublin the next afternoon. She offered me a choice of two nearby locations: Belfast Castle or the Shankill Road. I chose the Shankill Road.

It was the weekend of July 12th. This is a special time for the Protestant community in Northern Ireland, when they commemorate The Battle of the Boyne (1690), in which the Protestant William of Orange triumphed over the Catholic King James. Unlike July 4th in the United States, July 12th is not a celebration of overall unity between different people sharing the same land, but one of anger and division.

The Orange men were marching on the Shankill with lots of flags, banners, and music. People quickly gathered around to watch. I didn't understand the significance at the time, but everywhere I looked larger-than-life murals decorated the sides of buildings, expressing grief, hatred, and murder. Graphic pictures of men in black ski masks with guns pointing out at people passing by were proudly displayed on edifice walls for all to see.

Slowly I understood this was a silent war, a violence without guns or words purposely passed along to the next generation so they might take up the mantle. The illustrations screamed out in vivid colors of paint to the children growing up in that community, "remember what happened and do not forget." As a Jew, I very much received and understood the message, as well as the pain and anger and sense of injustice behind it.

Without a moment's hesitation I laid my hand on every image I saw, uttering whatever prayer came to mind. I had never encountered such deeply entrenched hatred and anger before. It shocked me and cut deep into my soul. When I finally boarded the train back to Dublin, waving goodbye to my newfound friends, hot tears kept pooling and spilling. My throat felt tight and swollen. What kind of insanity was being poured out through those colors and depictions, washing over all souls within reach, poisoning the young and uninformed with their pain and anger? What kind of generation would emerge from their shadows?

In that first encounter I saw the Northern Irish as a people scarred. Protestants and Catholics were passing their unhealed wounds down to their children and grandchildren, third and fourth generations and beyond. What or who could ever speak solace to the pain of such loss? It was clear to me the god of their anger thirsted for revenge, and the cycle would continue—demanding blood for blood.

The Shankill haunted me long after I returned home and moved on to other projects and tours.

In 2006 I traveled to Northern Ireland a second time to do some special concerts after which I would proceed to Dublin. During my time in Belfast I became acquainted with a missionary couple, Marvin and Gloria, who hoped to plant a Protestant church in the Catholic community of Belfast. They were informal house parents or overseers for the New Life Community House where I was staying, compliments of New Life Community Church. On one of my free days Marvin offered to tour me through some of the more scenic areas of the Northern Coast, since he had a car at his disposal. No small luxury.

It was another incredibly beautiful day, so we ventured out to see the castle at Carrick-Fergus. It is a Norman castle sitting right on the sea and is quite formidable looking. Old stone, mortar, canons, and the overwhelming smell of brine. After lunch we proceeded up the famous Antrim coast. We only got a little way into the drive when we were flagged down by three women and a man.

Their vehicle had stopped working and they needed a ride back into West Belfast, located on the Catholic side of what is known as The Peace Wall.

The first time I saw The Peace Wall was in 2004. It was erected in the late 60s as a temporary measure to quell violence during a time in Ireland known as The Troubles. It is the last standing partition still dividing communities in Europe, with gates that open and close at prescribed times.

Without a second's hesitation Marvin invited the four to pile in. Being born and raised in Los Angeles, which is not exactly known for openly trusting strangers, I wondered if that was a good idea. But Marvin immediately began witnessing to them about the Lord. Clearly this seemingly chance meeting was not a coincidence, as he and his wife had just started a church plant in West Belfast.

However, as things turned out, it was one of our passengers who did the lion's share of talking. Brenda was quite intoxicated and feeling very free. She intended to demonstrate how she could heal people and without so much as a *"Do you mind if I—"* she placed her hands on the sides of Marvin's head while he was driving.

It was a two-lane highway where we were, not very wide, and I rather emphatically reminded Brenda, "He's driving!"

She said, "Can you feel it?"

Marvin said, "I feel your hands."

"That's all?"

Brenda proved undaunted and demanded I surrender a hand so she could redeem herself. I cautiously extended my pinkie. She curled her fingers around it asking, "Do you feel that?"

"I feel your hands—that's all."

As we drove back to Belfast Marvin and I shared how flesh births flesh and only spirit can birth spirit, and how much God loves us all. In-between our hopeful witness to our new friends, Brenda held forth on evolution, how we are all God's children, and randomly yelled out the car window, "Kill the Brits!"

Brenda was unquestionably drunk, but impressively coherent nonetheless, and she posed a question I shall never forget. It is one of those queries which immediately exposes the heart of the one called upon to answer. Knowing I was Jewish she asked, "Did God ever love Hitler?"

How does any Jewish person begin to respond? It's almost, but not quite, like asking if God loves evil. The obvious difference is Hitler was a human being, created by the same One who made us all.

I thought about the first time I ever encountered anti-Semitism. It was after a long day at the flower shop. It was a December night around 8PM and it was Hannukah, the Feast of Lights. A car drove up in front of the shop where we were standing and the people yelled some kind of comment like, "You dirty Jews!" My mom, enraged, picked up a rock and threw it at them as they drove away. I had never seen her like that.

Some years later my parents made plans to take my brother and me to Europe for two weeks. It was a very big deal! New clothes, passports, and faraway places. I think it was my dad's way of catering to Mom. She wanted to see Italy and all the artwork of Michelangelo. She was our tour coordinator, and as it was still undecided exactly where else we would go on this vacation I seized the opportunity to ask, "Can we go to Germany? I hear it's a really beautiful country."

Mom stared hard at me. Her answer was immediate, concise, and non-negotiable. "Jews don't go to Germany."

That was the beginning and end of the conversation.

It was some time before I understood why. Like so many things my parents never discussed, they didn't talk about evil. I don't remember ever discussing the Holocaust with Mom, and that was the strongest allusion she ever made. But it was clear and powerful. It stayed with me.

Eventually I read books, beginning with *The Diary of Anne Frank,* and saw many movies that framed my understanding of what happened in Germany, and ignited a deep anger toward the evil of the Holocaust. We are, after all, a people deeply devoted to justice as we understand it, and I eventually came to understand Germany was not our friend.

I don't recall how I finally answered Brenda. I was still processing her question and would continue to do so for quite some time. But somewhere in the middle of that maze of information and emotion, there was a lull in the conversation—a stillness—and Brenda shared about her dad who had recently passed away. I could see her struggle with some emotion as she spoke and I laid my hand on her shoulder, asking to pray for her. For just an instant there was a tiny window of grace. She was quiet and thoughtful, but it was entirely over in the next moment. When we entered the Shankill (Protestant community in Belfast) she started yelling out the window again, "Kill the Brits!"

Brenda was loud, drunk, and vulgar. At the same time she was terribly wounded, vulnerable, and genuinely curious. Sometimes it is hard to see past our own filters and fears to find the actual people hiding behind their walls. God gave Marvin and me His vision that day, to see a little deeper than Brenda's façade so we could touch her soul.

I am haunted by a picture in my mind of holding out a single red rose in my hand, extended into darkness. Without shame, without defense, no argument or persuasion in my mouth, but choosing to be fully present and vulnerable before God and man, I am holding out a rose a sign of the love of God into a vortex of human pain and suffering and all its emotional train. I am powerless to make people believe the blood of Jesus can heal even the darkest corner of their pain. Each of us who choose to do so can only stand, with hand extended, offering a rose. And in that posture we are putting our own hearts before them as well.

(Journal—Sally Klein O'Connor)

4

THREE RED ROSES

After my first visit in 2007 I traveled to Poland again the following year. I stayed in Oswiecim for a conference entitled, *From Holocaust to Living Hope.* While there, I witnessed a profound exchange. The son of a notorious SS officer, along with his wife—both now born-again believers in Christ—washed the feet of a Jewish believing couple by the train tracks inside Birkenau, asking forgiveness for the sins of his father and their nation. I watched them hug each other in complete acceptance, and together raise the communion cup, blessing the wine and blessing us. As David says in the Psalms, "How good and how pleasant it is for brethren dwell together in unity." (Psalm 133:1)

After the conference ended, I moved out of my little dormitory room at the Center for Dialogue and Prayer, and stayed with Karen, who had been translating for many of the speakers. British by birth, Karen has a tremendous heart for the Polish people. She had befriended me earlier in the process of working out how I could attend the conference.

One night at her apartment I dreamed of red roses and, as strange as it seemed, felt I was supposed to give them to someone, but I didn't know whom. I remembered the previous year, when Evi and I wandered through Birkenau for the first time, and I noticed bouquets of red roses on the train tracks and by the crematoriums. Roses for the dead. The thought occurred to me then, what if, in this place, we gave roses to the living?

Later that day Karen and I borrowed bikes to ride out to the camp. On the way there I had the opportunity to ask some of the people who lived nearby why they chose to settle in such close proximity to this former concentration camp. It turned out many families were forced to evacuate by the Germans during the war and their lands and houses were confiscated. When it was all over, they wanted their properties back. Many had lived there for generations.

They didn't have much to say about what happened to the Jewish people, but they told me many Polish people were also killed. And after the war, they had nowhere to go, except back to the land that was theirs. That their houses now looked out on a place designated Memorial of Destruction, as the signs read, didn't seem to bother them. They wanted to live where they had put down roots. It was a lot to digest and I needed some time to walk through the camp again.

Birkenau is a strange mixture of the holy and profane. There is a deep stillness in the place, even when there are hundreds of people walking around. It's as if the ground itself bears silent witness to the ongoing history of sin and the evil that all human beings are capable of committing. It is a solemn reminder of the immeasurable depravity of man. But even as I was aware of the evil that created such a place, I could not ignore the powerful sense of God's presence, as if He, Himself, keeps vigil there.

Leaving through the gate at Birkenau, once again I caught sight of the houses nearby and could not ignore that Polish people were choosing to raise their families in such a place. I was angry at first, but somehow it turned around inside me and what occurred to me then was that I might give roses to some of those people living in the houses near Birkenau.

I asked Karen if she would purchase three long-stemmed red roses and three blank greeting cards. I sat outside the entrance waiting for her to return and started thinking about what to say in these cards.

My thoughts wandered, twisting around each other. Then I prayed. These are the words the Lord impressed on my heart to write:

A Rose of Remembrance.

Red for the blood of the people who died here

Red for the Savior's blood which was shed
for the blood of my people and your people

Red for His love, which makes
love between our people possible

Karen wrote it out in Polish, including the envelope, which read, "Because of love."

The first man we brought a rose to was drinking a beer in his front yard, which faced the entrance to Birkenau. He must have been in his early sixties. I wasn't quite sure what to do. I said, "Hallo! I'm from America and I'm Jewish and I want to give this to you." I handed him the rose and card as Karen translated for me. His face lit up. He was very surprised and exclaimed excitedly, "Nothing like this has ever happened to me."

He told us he had lived there forty years. He recounted seeing Jewish people parking their cars and walking past his house to enter Birkenau. The cars were everywhere, and there were so many people walking past him to go see the camp. He shared some of his story, then showed us his flowers and garden, and he let me take his picture. We must have spoken together for almost a half hour. I honestly didn't think Polish men talked that much! I think, in retrospect, we might have made him a little nervous.

The second man was building his house. It looked finished on the outside, but there was still a lot of work to do on the inside. He was a big guy, maybe in his forties, and Karen didn't think it would be appropriate to give him the card and flower because it seemed as if he hadn't lived there very long and he might not be receptive. But as we talked with him, he told us his family had all lived in the tiny shack on the lot next to his new house for years. I went back to our bikes to get a rose and card for him. While I was gone he related to Karen how for seventeen years he tried to obtain a permit to build a new house for his family on their land. And, in fact, he had not recovered all his property that was taken during the war, though he had received some compensation. As I rounded the corner, he told Karen, all this was because of the Jews, but added that he didn't hold it against them. Not knowing any Polish, I had no clue what he had said as I handed him the rose and card and introduced myself as an American who is Jewish. Timing is everything.

Karen caught me up on all he had shared with her while I was gone. He was quite open with his feelings, and after a while he asked me, "Why can't I have my land back?"

I said, "I can't imagine why you want to live in this place and raise your family here." I shared with him how I had wondered for some time about the people who lived so near the camp, pondering why anyone would want to put down roots near there. It didn't seem right to me. "After all," I said, "this is not a graveyard or a cemetery. This was the scene of a massacre."

I told him for us, as Jews, Birkenau was hard to look at. A place to remember death—a very painful and difficult memorial for us—which was why it was so hard to imagine anyone voluntarily choosing to live near it. He had never considered my viewpoint, just as I had not considered his. I informed him not only was I Jewish, but also a believer in Jesus. Even as I spoke it began to occur to me that maybe people living here could be considered a redeeming act, like Spring coming after a very long Winter. Life after death.

Without fully knowing what I was doing, I picked up a stone from his walkway, a token of his new home, and pronounced a simple benediction, "May the Lord bless your house and all who live there—and may it be a place of joy!"

As we approached the last home, an older man in his sixties or seventies was outside fixing his car. He didn't want to be bothered at first, and Karen thought he looked at us pretty suspiciously. But when I told him I was Jewish and from America, then offered the rose to him as a gift, he seemed really shocked. It appeared he might cry or get angry—I couldn't tell which. At first he wouldn't accept it. He wanted me to give it to his wife, but I insisted it was for him. He eventually received it with some reluctance, then excused himself and got his wife. She read the card and was very moved. She invited us to walk with her to where the train tracks crossed right next to their land. She asked Karen if we would pray for her. I saw great regret and shame in her face. After our "amen" there were tears in her eyes.

Even after hearing some of their stories, I still struggled with why anyone would want to raise families or live their lives in a house whose windows overlook one of the bleakest moments of human history. But I realize now that this is not a question for which I need an answer. It is not why God led me there that day.

Kindness is a type of seed. The Bible says of God that it's His kindness that leads us to repentance. And this is what I felt the Lord turning me toward. Because of God's love in my life, I found the grace to extend His kindness to each of the people living in those three houses near Birkenau. My hope is that, even after the roses withered and the cards were misplaced, each would remember the kindness God gave me to share with them that day.

"Perhaps we fear that if we forgive we might discover that the person who perpetrated that great evil against us is more like us than we care to admit."

(Forgive and Forget: Healing the Hurts We Don't Deserve by Lewis B. Smedes)

"We love because He first loved us."

(1 John 4:19)

The ability to love truly, unselfishly, is in us only because we turned to Him who loves us so richly. Unfathomably and infinitely, this deposit, this ore of love is in us forever as our hope and our indictment/conviction. He loves us so deeply and profoundly unconditionally that the tiniest fragment of that love lodged in our system can overthrow our stony hearts and make us truly human... divinely human.

(Sally Klein O'Connor—Journal—10-16-2006)

5

BEING PRESENT

On a birthday some years ago I ended up in therapy because my regular appointment just happened to coincide that year with my special day. My husband, Michael, warned me that going might not be a good idea if I hoped to enjoy the rest of the day. But I was sure I could handle whatever surfaced. I had a fairly good rapport with our counselor and thought it might help my time of reflection on this particular day.

She said it as an afterthought, a footnote, just before the last grains of sand in the 50-minute glass ran out. It was part of her closing prayer. It sprang full-blown from left field, completely unexpected, and stung me deeply, producing immediate denial.

She prayed I would not treat Michael (and others) as an object instead of a person.

That had never occurred to me before. But try as I might I couldn't shake her comment. As the week wore on, her words began ruthlessly applying themselves to my world. I noticed items that had not been on my radar prior to her prayer. Moments when I wasn't fully present to my girls. As they told me about their day, the flow of information passed through my ears into my brain, but my heart was elsewhere. I responded to their questions and conversation appropriately enough, but I was already thinking ahead to what was next.

School mornings, when everyone was running late, I was all about what needed to be done. Making sure Dusty and Bonnie got up relatively on time, preparing Bonnie's lunch, helping Shannon dress, breakfast, Bonnie's hair, Shannon's hair, shoes and sweaters. Did everyone brush their teeth? Did Dusty get her lunch? Out the door, in the car—was everyone buckled? Bonnie's tape player, Shannon's toys, Dusty's iPod, my radio—was everybody happy? Or if not happy, quiet? Entertained? Or at least distracted enough for me to continue what *I* was doing?

One afternoon, as I was negotiating another in a series of daily "misunderstandings" between our pre-teen Bonnie and our post-toddler Shannon, I realized that, although I was handling the situation pretty well, I was not really caring for them. My entire goal was to contain the screaming and help them understand each other without necessarily finding out how each one really felt. Truth be told, I didn't want to take the time to ferret out their feelings. Too much effort. It was just one more task needing to be addressed before dishes and cooking dinner so that maybe, sometime after they were safely tucked in bed, I could watch a movie or work on my music. That's right. It was all about *me* and *my* time.

I began to realize there were occasions when all the people and events in my life felt more like obstacles to hurdle over or crawl under, so that I could eventually get to myself and address what *I* wanted. Not a pretty picture.

Soon after I came to faith in 1984, I started working for a ministry. The founder was an older Jewish man who had come to faith in a Pentecostal environment. While working there I encountered many different leaders of churches and other ministries associated with that particular denomination, which was the covering for the ministry I worked for. It seemed fairly common to speak of how many souls were saved in a service.

Still brand new in Jesus and unfamiliar with itinerant ministry, I often wondered whether the people who talked about souls being saved had any concern for the rest of the person. Often, the number of salvations seemed more important than the names of the people who carried those now-saved souls within them. I couldn't help but wonder if the actual individuals whose names had been added to the mailing list really mattered to those who counted and catalogued them for the sake of the Kingdom.

Soon after, my husband, Michael, and I began Improbable People Ministries based on the songs and stories we felt the Lord had put on our hearts to share. While we didn't count souls, I made almost no effort to remember the names of people we encountered during our concert tours. It seemed an impossible task. So I would hold onto a name just long enough to share and pray with them in the place we met. Then, like fragile leaves that suddenly disconnect and slowly float down from trees in autumn, I would let their name detach and drift from my mind. It was not a completely conscious act, but one based on self-preservation. Attached to those names and faces were stories, many filled with pain. I had trouble connecting to each individual beyond that particular instance without processing their stories and pain through my own less than perfect emotional grid.

In 1 Chronicles there are more unpronounceable names listed per page than in any other book in the Bible. It is often tedious for that reason. But when I have prayerfully read those names, not just skimmed over them, I have often been struck by the realization God knew each person. They had a unique place in His plan, and their names were important enough to include in His word to the world. They were not simply a means to an end, human stepping-stones to help us cross a span of years to the next superhero in God's story. They were not a nameless, faceless crowd to their Maker. They were forefathers and predecessors, for some of us by race, and most of us by faith, grafted into that all too human lineage.

Clearly, God does not view us as objects. To Him we are individuals. Consider that many of us would not even know about a man called Jabez if God did not see him as someone worth including in 1 Chronicles 4—by name. But I think it is in the nature of sin to deface our humanity, either little by little or in large chunks.

I live in Los Angeles. The traffic in this small country of a city is as bad as it gets anywhere in the rest of the United States. There really is no guarantee at any time of day that you will avoid traffic. There may be certain moments when the odds are better that you will find a clear stretch of road between your point of departure and your destination, but that is all.

Imagine driving to your destination. You have the radio/CD player set on your favorite selection and the temperature in the car is perfect. You happily anticipate what awaits you at the end of the drive, when suddenly you slam your foot down on the brake pedal, barely avoiding the rear end of the car that checked into your lane without warning.

What do you feel?

Do you give them the standard middle digit salutation? Do you wish you could? Do you let your horn do the talking? Or is all the commentary in your head? In that moment does the driver as an individual even matter—or are you only aware of their action and how it affected *you?* Are they still human or more of an inconvenience, an annoyance—if you are trying to be polite—or just a flat-out idiot? Perhaps they no longer seem human at all but something that is getting in your way and deserves to be written off for inconveniencing you.

When men indulge in pornography it has been said the women in the pictures cease to exist for those men as female individuals and become objects of desire whose sole purpose is to fulfill men's lusts. The word is objectification.

When one nation subjugates another there is a loss of humanity, not only for those who are oppressed, but those who are the oppressors. They are denying a basic truth that nevertheless bonds us together because that is simply how God designed us. We are unique beings, made in the image of an all-powerful and ever-merciful Maker.

In the moment we see some people as "less than" or even as objects, we diminish their humanity—and our own as well.

When Nazi Germany slaughtered 11 million, they gassed and cremated a portion of their own souls. But they had so disconnected from those who had once been friends, neighbors, even family, that they only saw them as a threat to their survival as a race and nation. Objects and obstacles that needed to be numbered and removed, in order to achieve their perception of the greater good.

But after the war, my parents and most of their generation who were Jewish, stopped seeing Germans as individuals, but viewed them collectively as a people who were a threat to *their* survival. Many Germans were portrayed as monsters—sometimes fools like Colonel Klink in the old TV show *Hogan's Heroes*—and we were always their victims. At that time, it never crossed my mind whether or not the Germans suffered. If it had, I would have felt whatever pain and loss the Germans endured was more than earned and justified and, even then, not enough. As a Jew, I saw them only as perpetrators of great evil and never gave a second thought to the consequences Germany experienced because of their choices in World War II. It never occurred to me that they also might be victims of a greater evil.

Our humanity is our basic connection with God, and it sets us apart from the rest of creation—the realization we are made in His likeness. But there is so much in and around us hardening our hearts to the reality of that miracle. So we often treat ourselves and others as objects, disconnecting from our humanity and theirs, like autumn leaves from their branches.

When we connect to Jesus, He begins to green and grow us, restore us to the people God intended—capable of a love that lays its life down for another.

Jesus said: "I tell you the truth, whatever you did for one of the least of these brothers of mine, you did for me." (Matthew 25:40).

Hitler and the Nazis portrayed the Jewish people as vermin, rats that needed to be exterminated. The Germans removed all dignity from the Jews, reducing them to a plague they needed to eradicate. The

Nazis understood themselves as ridding the world of an unwanted element. It didn't seem to matter that the particular group involved included brothers and sisters, husbands and wives, friends and neighbors. Every time they betrayed those relationships in the name of house cleaning, their souls became slightly colder—a little harder, more numb, a little less human.

I wonder now if we, as Jews, have not done something similar in spirit to the Germans, lifting their evil onto a kind of pedestal and making them monsters instead of men.

"By turning Eichmann into an unforgivable monster, we set him beyond human accountability, beyond good and evil. Nobody forgives the devil. Why not? It is because he is beyond the struggle between good and evil; he is only pure evil, and therefore we set him outside the possibility of being forgiven." (*Forgive and Forget: Healing the Hurts We Don't Deserve* by Lewis B. Smedes)

In our zeal to make sure a holocaust never happens again, have we forgotten *their* humanity? Have we lost sight of our common mortal struggles and flaws before God? Is it possible we have become prideful in our righteous anger, as if we considered ourselves incapable of ever thinking *those* thoughts or committing *those* actions, which might lead to something as horrific as the Holocaust?

"Forgetting is something time alone takes care of, but forgiveness is an act of volition, and only the sufferer is qualified to make the decision."

Simon Wiesenthal

"Forgiveness to me means that whatever was done to me it is no longer causing me such pain that I cannot be the person that I want to be."

Eva Kor

"Nobody can make you forgive. Only a free person can choose to live with an uneven score. Only free people can choose to start over with someone who has hurt them. Only a free person can live with accounts unsettled. Only a free person can heal the memory of hurt and hate."

(*Forgive and Forget: Healing the Hurts We Don't Deserve* by Lewis B. Smedes)

6

NEVER AGAIN

"Never Again" reads the Jewish Memorial at Dachau. Two words. They are both an epitaph to what will always be a shameful piece of mankind's history and a somber warning to future generations. And yet, in the more than seventy years since the victory and liberation of 1945, how has the world responded to those words?

In Poland, immediately after the war, violence broke out in many villages. One of the more well-known examples being the 1946 pogrom in Kielce. In many of these smaller Polish communities Jewish survivors returned home to find former friends and neighbors now stealing and destroying Jewish property and murdering Jewish people. In the Soviet Union anti-Semitism continued unchecked.

Years later, in Rwanda, one tribe of people wiped out a million of another in the country's brutal civil war. The Protestants and the Catholics in Northern Ireland have been at it for centuries. The Jews and Arabs are brothers by blood who cannot stop fighting. The Crips and Bloods, and many other gangs continue warring against each other in the inner cities of the U.S. Bloodshed and violence between people and nations persists unabated, and I can't help wondering how futile are those words, "Never Again?"

It would seem that as long as individuals live on the face of the earth bloodshed and violence will continue. On some level it is simply the legacy of sin. That many of us want to stop it is admirable. But what is accomplished by stating what so obviously seems, on a world-wide scale, impossible? Isn't there something more to do than building monuments to massacres in the hope that we won't do it again? When I first began exploring questions like these, I encountered a Jewish woman named Eva Kor.

Michael and I love watching movies. It's part of how we relax and unwind. Watching online has become a convenient way to enjoy theatre at home. One night, Mike told me about a film he had seen listed—a documentary called *Forgiving Doctor Mengele*.

Eva Kor is one of the few remaining Jewish survivors of Auschwitz. During the war she lost all her family except her twin sister. She and her twin were experimented on by Dr. Mengele, who permanently blocked one of her sister's kidneys from maturing with the rest of her body. After liberation in 1945 they both moved to Israel. Her sister remained, but Eva traveled to the states. Years later Eva set out on a courageous quest to discover if she could help her twin recover from the effects of Mengele's experiment. She wanted to find out if the doctor kept notes, in the hope they might discover how the effects of his handiwork could be reversed.

The first time Eva returned to Auschwitz she was paralyzed with fear, to the point she couldn't function. "Anytime I thought about a German, not a Nazi, I would say I hate those Germans. And when you say I hate those Germans there is a feeling inside your guts that you hate them."

But in the course of her research she met Dr. Hans Munch, an ex-Nazi camp doctor from Auschwitz. Meeting Dr. Munch was a game changer for Eva Kor.

She discovered he was human.

After the war, ex-SS Doctor Hans Munch was acquitted because of the testimony given by several Jews that he helped them survive by keeping them in the infirmary long after they had actually recovered.

Dr. Munch said "All the memories of Auschwitz were such that I had no great joy… in my freedom." He told Eva that people being gassed was a recurring nightmare he lived with.

"I was absolutely flabbergasted that Nazis had nightmares about Auschwitz," said Eva. Who could blame her for thinking this way? Who could blame any Jewish person affected by the Holocaust—and on some level that was all of us—for it affecting our view of every German we ever met? The unspoken question was, can people do such horrific things to each other and still be human?

Upon meeting Dr. Munch, she discovered he was not a monster but a *mensch* (a real person) with some of the most profound regret Eva ever encountered. It was a wonder to her. While he wasn't able to locate any of Dr. Mengele's notes, he agreed to sign a paper bearing personal witness of the use of the Zyklon B gas for killing the prisoners in the camps. He signed the paper in the presence of several other survivors at Auschwitz, on the 50th anniversary of the liberation.

After returning home to the states, Eva Kor contemplated how she could show her gratitude to Dr. Munch for his brave declaration. For ten months, every morning, she reminded herself of the task at hand; find a way to thank Dr. Munch for his witness. And one day, she stumbled on it. She decided to write him a letter of amnesty.

Inconceivable! Fellow survivors were greatly offended, even outraged. How could Eva forgive Dr. Munch for his part in her family's murder and the Holocaust? It wasn't hers to forgive!

But she did forgive, and in the process found profound healing and release for herself. As Eva says, "A victim has no choice in the matter. All victims are hurt, helpless and hopeless. I discovered a power I didn't know." The moment she decided to write Dr. Munch a letter of amnesty, she learned the power of forgiving, and that set her free. She was no longer a victim. She released Dr. Munch from her judgment, and in the process, to her great surprise, obtained her own liberty.

She was then challenged by a friend to forgive Dr. Mengele and all the other Nazis.

Eva shared, "After forgiving the Nazis, a huge burden of pain was lifted from my shoulders. Now I can go into the camp, I can touch the barbed wire and it's no longer going to kill me. So I am now a free human being... I am no longer hurting. I am not going to hold onto the pain just to fit into a certain category."

In April 2015 Eva posted on her Facebook page in regard to a more current event:

Today I met Oskar Groening, the 93-year-old former SS who is on trial in Germany. I introduced myself and reached out to shake his hand. The strangest thing happened. He was trying to say something as he was sitting sideways in his chair. He turned white and fell backwards, not saying a word. He was holding onto my arm so he did not hit the floor. At that moment he was not a Nazi but an old man who fainted and I was trying to save him from falling...

Eva continued posting on her timeline over the next few days, a little more of her interaction with Oskar Groening:

Today after the afternoon session of the court, I went up to Oskar Groening.

He wanted to stand up. I said, "Please don't, we do not want a repetition of last time." I just shook his hand and said, "I appreciate the fact that you are willing to come here and face us. But I would like you to appeal to the old Nazis who are still alive to come forward and address the problem of neo-Nazis in Germany today. Because these young misguided Germans who want Hitler and fascism to come back they will not listen to Eva Kor or any other survivor. You can tell them you were in Auschwitz, you were involved with the Nazi party, and it was a terrible thing."

As I was talking to him, he grabbed me and gave me a kiss on the cheek. Well, I probably wouldn't have gone that far, but I guess it is better than what he would have done to me 70 years ago.

I am asking a question: What do we want in the future? Do we want to keep pointing fingers and the accused stay in one corner and the accuser stay in the other corner and they never connect? How will that work out?

When tragic things happen, we have to sit down and discuss, what are the options for the victims and for the perpetrators? Most people are only here in court to accuse him of things he has already admitted. So now what? I don't think we should raise a statue in his honor, but he can serve as a good example to young people that what he participated in was terrible, that it was wrong, and that he is sorry that he was part of it. Now there is a message that has some usefulness for society.

If I had it my way, the dialogue between the survivors and perpetrators would have started a long time ago. And it would have helped the survivors cope and maybe heal themselves, but even more so not to pass the pain on to their children.

I continue to be amazed by her testimony because this is a woman who publicly states she does not believe in God. The Creator is not part of her worldview, at least at the time of our initial conversation. Maybe she became angry with Him, blaming Him for what happened during WWII. Perhaps she lost sight of Him—as so many did in the Shoah—because He did not rescue them. Be that as it may, she came to grips with something absolutely basic to the Christian faith, which many long-time Christians continue to struggle with profoundly—forgiveness. She, who does not believe in God, has forgiven a people who were part of one of the most dreadful chapters in human history.

Amazingly, she even has a kind of compassion for the Germans. As Eva puts it, when the Jews look back at World War II they have nothing to be ashamed of as a people, but when the Germans look back they will always see the Holocaust.

Forgiveness is underestimated. Eva puts it this way, "Forgiveness is a seed for peace. Anger or revenge is a seed for war."

May we never forget, but may God help us find a way to forgive.

I met Sally at the conference in Oswiecim last year. She came afterwards to visit Nürnberg and we went together to Dachau. It was typical for God that I had a breakdown in front of the first crematorium on German earth and Sally as a Jew was consoling me. After that we had seen the beautiful garden that God made in Dachau at the palace. I could start to realize that God has given us Germans a chance to live, although we did the most cruel thing which I could think of to his people. I'm very thankful that God gives us Germans, who always feel our sin, relief of it and that the shame which is there for every German generation could be taken away by the blood of Jesus. My experience is, that this could only (be) given to us by Jews, who speak to us and pray with and for us...

(Dagmar Menzel, Nuremberg, Germany 2008)

Giving out red roses in each town may very well be the most challenging thing any of us have ever done. It seems to be both an intimate thing as well as bold. Even though I had some experience of it when I gave out three red roses last year near Birkenau, it is still hard to imagine what it will feel like to hold out a red rose to a stranger in the town square or market place of Oswiecim, Dachau, or Bergen and Belsen. Will there be smiles and tears, angry words and hostile looks, distrust? I have wondered all these things and realize there is nothing I can do to prepare for how people will receive our gifts, and ourselves, but choose to love as Jesus loves unconditionally.

(Sally Klein O'Connor—Journal—2009)

7

LOVE IS WALKING

It was Jesus who led me to Poland and Germany the first time in 2007, again in 2008, and finally, in 2009 with a team of people and a vision. Quite honestly, only Jesus could have brought me there to extend myself in His love. And the surprising thing is, although it began in my mind as a burden, the experience was not like that at all. I felt such joy in places I had only associated with pain because I sensed the presence of God and His love for the people around us. But then it is Jesus who reaches out through us every time we extend our hearts beyond those way-too-comfortable boundaries of our faith, to touch the hand of someone broken and forgotten. He does not forget nations or individuals. As Hagar said of Him in her particular wilderness, "You are the God who sees me." (Genesis 16:13)

We are our own limitation. Afraid to see where God is looking, afraid to hear what He might be saying, we turn away from the opportunity to realize our true purpose in this life—what we were created for. Instead, we choose to color carefully inside the lines of our understanding of Christianity as we decide it applies to us, and our faith slowly withers and dies.

It is Jesus who tells me through Paul's writings: "So from now on we regard no one from a worldly point of view. Though we once regarded Christ in this way, we do so no longer." (2 Corinthians 5:16)

That means all our acceptable, justifiable, and all too predictable religious prejudice is not OK with the One we say we love. We are not supposed to think about anyone in the way we once did before we came into an intimate walk with the Son. We are called to love—not judge. That is God's job and He says, "Mercy triumphs over judgment." (James 2:13)

Loving with the kind of unconditional passion God has for us is nowhere in our human DNA. Some of us learn to judge just to survive our situations and that is how we protect ourselves. I know. I am chief among sinners on this issue.

But "God **so** loved…"

How deep, how wide, how high, how long is the quality of that love described in those two little letters—*so*? We have been *so* loved and are called to love others as we have been loved, and that is exactly what happened during our time in Poland and Germany with the first *A Tour of Roses (ATOR)*.

> (We) sang and worshiped in the town square as well as the marketplace as we gave out roses… the presence of God came down and we were enveloped in the Glory of God. It was like a piece of heaven.
>
> People stopped to listen, some were moved to tears, and we sensed how God was touching hearts. Sharing the love of Jesus has never been so easy! One man I spoke to just stood there and we were able to pray for him and lead him to the Lord—right there on the streets. Amazing!
>
> (Mark Warwick, Krakow, Poland)

We ran out of roses at the market place and bought another hundred. We gave those away in a heartbeat. One team member, Vincent, was so thrilled he offered to buy more—and we gave those out also. He was ready to buy another round—and I have to admit being able to give with such freedom and joy is kind of addicting—but I reminded him we were just here to plant some seeds in people's hearts.

People came to the concert—about 250. They heard and felt something in what we shared through the roses and worship, and they wanted more. Never mind I could barely pronounce the name of their town, let alone speak a word of Polish. Never mind that they didn't know a single song I sang. Never mind they had never heard of me before. None of that mattered. They were hungry and the Lord had put loaves and fishes into our hands.

They were grateful for the love and kindness that God poured out through us during those two days. I think it surprised them we had actually purposed to come and reach out to them in their town—this place so seemingly God-forsaken because of its history. We were not—as so many others have done—just staying in the town so we could go see the camps and museums. We had specifically come to be with the people of the town and they were deeply touched. Several times during the concert they broke out in applause over something I shared, and like children who know when they have tasted something good, they wanted more.

Later, we shared the apples and honey of Rosh Hashanah with the people of Oswiecim—to bless them with a good and sweet new year, and it was powerful. They were grateful to partake with us. It was a holy thing, like breaking the bread of communion together.

(Sally's Journal)

You know this kind of thing amazes me that in THIS place—this place of death, God chooses to heal. God is a God of redemption—He wants to turn every evil into blessing.

(Mark Warwick)

In Nuremberg, where Hitler had been venerated in an almost worshipful fashion, we had an amazing time of praise and prayer at Zeppelin Field, reciting the ancient Hebrew declaration of faith, the Sh'ma, in the very spot where Hitler had spoken hate. And then we sat down and took communion together.

We had a great and blessed time to pray where the altars of evil were: in the middle of the former Congress hall and on the stairs of the Zeppelin-grandstand, where Hitler spoke his hate-speeches. The praise of God filled the air, sung by Jews, Polish, Americans, English and German people. The atmosphere changed so that we could breathe.

(Dagmar Menzel, Nuremberg, Germany)

Soon after we traveled to Dachau to worship in the camp and hand out roses in the town. Dachau has existed since 800 AD. Few people who visit spend much time in the community itself, choosing to focus solely on the infamous concentration camp right next door. On the streets the Germans were reserved and skeptical— very different from the openness we experienced in Poland.

The morning of the concert in Dachau we gave out roses in an older part of town and the reaction was quite different. It was as if people were protecting themselves, never thinking for a moment that the rose could really be a gift for them. There must be strings attached. One woman walked away shaking her head, assuring us there had to be a price for receiving a rose. "Geschenk," we told them. It's a present! It's for you, because God loves you and me! And then their faces changed—softened into smiles and wonder. Could we really mean that this gift is for them? Yes! Rich Mullins said it well... "There's a wideness in God's mercy I cannot find in my own..."

(Sally's Journal)

I have this feeling that something amazing happened. Something unique breaking through and not only for me personally, but most of all for people from cities we were handing roses out. It was like opening doors that kept being locked 'til this time.

(Magda Balcerak, Warsaw, Poland)

Last night no one knew how many people would actually come to the ballroom of the Palace at Dachau... About 300 people came to the concert... Inna Pikman, Vladimir's wife, led us in worship and then I shared. Toward the end of my concert, Vladimir came up and talked about how the Holocaust is a scar between the Jews and Germans. That when Jews think about Germany they think about the Holocaust and when Germans think about Jews they think about the Holocaust. And Vladimir said, that is not all there is! It was amazing! Afterward, the pastor of the church who had been very cautious about what we were doing was smiling so hard I thought his face would split in two. There was so much love... It was truly as if God rained down His mercy from heaven on us last night. So much love expressed between Jews and Germans and even my Polish friend, Magda, was totally blessed to see such love. I don't even know what to say about this—except this is so obviously God's heart for these people to heal and not to live under condemnation and shame.

(Sally's Journal)

The little town of Bergen was our last stop on the tour. I have to smile when I think about how desperate I must have seemed at times, trying to find someone to connect to in this town. At one point in planning for the outreach in Dachau, someone gave me the number of a German woman to call who knew an Englishman, Philip, who had put together a Christian event a year or two before. In order to communicate the phone number she had to recite the digits in Spanish, because I couldn't understand a single word of German at that time and she spoke no English at all. Fortunately for me I still remembered my numbers in Spanish.

In Bergen I called and emailed the town council. I don't remember how many times I called, left messages, or emailed, but eventually a woman responded to me in English by email. Katharina said the council was very touched by my request to do a free concert in their town and to hand out roses on the streets. She explained they had decided to build a small stage in the park, complete with a little tent covering and benches for the evening event. It was hard for them all to wrap their minds around the idea that Jewish people wanted to come to their community to bless them.

It took hours to drive from Dachau to Bergen, but when we arrived we were warmly welcomed. The next day, as we began handing out roses, people were smiling practically everywhere we walked. Katharina had placed beautiful posters all over the town advertising *A Tour of Roses* and the concert.

They put together a beautiful stage, complete with special lighting and sound system. My friend, Dagmar, translated for me, and all the lyrics for the songs were up on a screen translated into German. It was a cool night, even for that part of Germany in the fall, but about 200 people came out for the concert. It was pretty amazing!

We made sure everyone received a little tapered candle to hold for a special part of the concert. Near the end, I invited us to not only remember together, the friends and family of Jews and Germans that were lost during the war, but to lift our candles in the hope of peace to come. We turned out all the lights in the audience area and dimmed the stage as people passed the light from candle to candle and I sang *Oseh Shalom*.

May He who makes peace in the heavens, grant peace to us and to all Israel, and let us say Amen.

LOVE IS WALKING

Pictures of a people, nameless faces
Where did all of them go?
Piles of their shoes, still with laces
Doesn't anyone know?
Roses on the tracks, rocks on the gravestones
We cry, "Never Again."
I can't help but wonder if time
Will ever heal the pain
Love is walking
Love is calling
Flowers lean into His wake
A fragrance sweet released
With ev'ry breath He takes
Love is walking
Love is calling
Through these fields of hate
Where tears and ashes still mix
And touch and wait
Scars upon the land bear silent witness
To a sin once concealed
Can there be redemption in this generation
For a wound that won't heal?
I read about the rain that falls like a blessing
On good and bad men the same
I'm wondering if Your mercy
Can wash away the shame
Love is walking
Love is calling
To hearts still broken by loss
There's a healing found only in the cross
Love is walking
Love is calling…

8

THE MAN IN THE MONSTER

"If you, O Lord, kept a record of sins,
O Lord, who could stand?
But with you there is forgiveness;
therefore you are feared."

(Psalm 130:3-4)

"When we declare an evil person to be beyond the pale of
forgiveness, we create a monster who does not even need to be
forgiven—a monster is excused from judgment by the fact
that he or she is beyond humanity."

(Forgive and Forget: Healing the Hurts We Don't Deserve by
Lewis B. Smedes)

Long ago, but not so far away, I lived in a very nice house in Studio City, CA. Our backyard consisted of a ¾ acre hill with just enough flatland to eventually create a swimming pool for my little brother and me. We loved acting out adventures. I usually mapped out the stories for our imaginary exploits and we would pretend all over the hill, in the pool, and around the deck all through the summer. There was great sweetness in our time together, but there were also some shadows.

Dad worked hard six days a week and stayed home on Sundays. Mom would take his place, handling things at the shop while he tried to rest at home. I guess we were not very conducive to resting because he labeled us "wild Indians." Dad had very little patience for the kind of adventures my brother and I enjoyed. He didn't have much grace for our imaginings. Inevitably there would come a moment during his Sunday Sabbath where my brother or I would cross a line and he would lose his temper. Rage would transform him. I still remember how the kids on the block would call him "The Monster." They never came over to our house on Sundays.

Ironically, every Saturday afternoon my mom and brother would sit in front of the TV for hours, totally engrossed, watching B-horror movies like the black and white version of *Godzilla*. I skulked in the corners of the TV room trying not to watch, but often in vain as I would eventually be sucked into the story's crude devices, gripped with suspense and paralyzing fear. At that point it was impossible to leave until the monster died. Unfortunately, not all those movies I watched ended so decisively. Cliffhangers were a popular choice in those days, like *The Blob,* with Steve McQueen. At the end, the people transport the blob to the North Pole where it's frozen forever unless, of course, climate change occurs.

In those years I had a recurring dream I could never figure out. It always began pleasantly enough. On a sunny day, I was in the passenger seat of a car driving along with someone I knew—someone I trusted—when I noticed the road looked strangely familiar. A little further on I recognized our route would lead directly to The Land of the Monsters. I pleaded with the person driving to turn around because I was sure we were traveling to The Land of the Monsters. But whoever was behind the steering wheel never believed me. They were certain that where they were going wasn't The Land of the Monsters. As the seconds ticked by, it became increasingly obvious we were heading directly there and I could do nothing about it. The dream ended at some point after we arrived. I always woke up terrified.

Michael and I started therapy to work on our marriage when I was in my forties. During our first session the Lord showed me that dream was about my father and me. One moment he was fine, I could talk to him, he was reasonable, things were good—a sunny day, not a cloud in the sky. And then, suddenly, everything would change. I was in The Land of the Monsters. I couldn't talk to him at all because he had become one of them. I was powerless to stop him until our punishment was over and his rage was spent. I hated my father for a very long time.

My dad and I had a history of arguing. For something so incredibly futile, we became very good at it. We instinctively knew all the moves. It was a dance ending the same way every time—anger and rage on both sides. It was not pretty, but it was ours. It had become a strange, sad bonding ritual between us.

In 1978 my parents' marriage ended after 30-something years. About six months later my brother, their only son, died at the age of 18.

Within the first year of becoming a believer in Jesus I was confronted with the issue of forgiveness concerning my feelings about my dad. I was still, for the most part, basking in the blissful state of my newfound faith in Messiah. As I saw it early on, forgiveness was something God did for us through the atoning work of His Son. I had not yet grasped it was also something expected of those who claimed to be His. I was still reading past those verses, not yet snagged by the little barbs in some of their hooks. I was dancing on the surface, unaware of the great deep just beyond what I could see.

I harbored a lot of resentment toward my father for some of the things he did to me, my brother, and my mom, as well as those things he didn't do that I saw other kids experience with their dads. His way of expressing love to us, as his family, was to work as hard as he knew how, earning as much money as he could so we could have almost everything we wanted. But Dad didn't know how to express love in a personal way—especially to my brother and me. He didn't know how to just be with us. And it frustrated him that we didn't respond in the way he expected. He didn't understand why we didn't appreciate his sacrifice, and we didn't understand why he wouldn't spend more time and attention on us. As the years went by there were only more misunderstandings, continually furthering the emotional distance between us.

One day he was visiting the house in Studio City where I grew up. A few months before my brother died, Mom had formally asked Dad to leave the house, saying she could no longer live with him. He never tried to move back in, but he often visited. And while I was staying at the house we would talk now and then. But for me, every conversation with my father at that time represented an opportunity to get back at him verbally for all the wrongs I felt he had done. This exchange started out no differently than any other, but wound up in an entirely different arena. As we started to argue a question surfaced in my mind, *Is this what your faith is about?* As brand new as I was to the teachings of Jesus, I understood that fighting with my father, or anyone for that matter, was not part of following the Lord.

"I'm going to my room now," I muttered as I walked out of the kitchen.

It was the longest walk over the shortest distance I have ever taken. It took forever to reach the door of my room off the garage. Once I was safely inside, several realizations hit me at once. The most powerful one helped me see that I had long since stopped seeing Dad as a person—an actual human being. When I was small, he was a monster to me in his rage, and as an adult he became a list of wrongs both real and perceived. But I had completely forgotten who he was as a man. Instead, I had buried his humanity under an ever-growing list of crimes I held him personally accountable for. And so, whenever I interacted with Dad that list was always present, within arm's reach in my heart and mind, just waiting for the first wrong word to open up the file in bold 24-point font. Anger was the only emotion we shared. It colored all our conversations. But that day everything changed.

The Lord reminded me of his humanity and invited me to love him. I began by saying the words I had wanted all my life to hear my father say to me: "I love you, Dad."

He responded, "I love you too!"

It was the very first time I can recall my dad telling me he loved me. It wasn't something he grew up with in his family. Hearing those words from his lips brought healing.

As Dad and I became friends he experienced the reality of my love and forgiveness toward him and a seed was planted in my father that I believe ultimately led him to faith in his Messiah, Jesus, at the ripe old age of 82. He told me many times along that road he knew it was because of my faith that we had finally become close. But a seed was also planted in me that day. One that revealed itself over several years. It was the idea that no human being was ever created to be a monster, and the power of God's love is such that it can turn monsters back into men. This is what the Kingdom of God is all about, that we who are sinners become saints and monsters become men.

9

JEDWABNE

"What would you do if your own name was a bad word?"

(Desperauex by Kate Decamillo)

You are a beautiful rose that Adonai (the Lord) has created. He sees past your thorns. Give them up to Him, Adonai only sees your beauty, His intended creation at the end of your journey. Bloom now for Adonai! In my prayers.

(Jeanne Davis, California—a blessing for Jedwabne)

I love roses. They are some of the most beautiful flowers God ever designed. They are also, in many ways, a metaphor for deeply wounded people: Beauty amid thorns. And let me tell you, some of the most beautiful, intensely fragrant roses I ever stripped thorns from caused me to bleed the most. But that's how it often is on this broken planet—some of the most attractively adorned and vividly colored creatures may also be the most poisonous. The toughest people may house the most tender hearts.

I was in Bethlehem in January 2015 to explore the possibility of bringing *A Tour of Roses* to one of the refugee camps. A Palestinian man, who had newly come to faith, responded to my idea of bringing roses by saying, "We need food and money, not roses."

I am always daunted when someone says something like that because there is nothing practical in what we are doing. Of course, food is a basic necessity and money is always helpful, but this is not what the Lord spoke into me. He called me to give out roses in dark and colorless places, to hard and hurting hearts, and even those who are indifferent, because He is the one true hope that can heal every heart. The roses symbolize that truth.

In 2010 I witnessed just how powerful, visually and spiritually, a few hundred roses could be in a small community like Jedwabne, Poland. In that small farming village, the very young and old still contend with the shame and anger of a massacre that happened over 70 years ago but is still an issue today.

Two memorials mark the history. The first is in the town square, a painful reminder to the more long-term residents of their Polish neighbors who were deported to Siberia, most of whom never returned. The other marker stands knee-deep in weeds, half-forgotten and mostly ignored, on the edge of Jedwabne, as a stark reminder of Jews, one-time citizens, friends and neighbors, who were murdered without mercy.

For many years the inscription on the second marker declared the massacre was accomplished by German soldiers occupying the town during the war:

Site of the Suffering of the Jewish Population.
The Gestapo and the Nazi Gendarmerie Burned Alive 1600 People
July 10, 1941.

But as a new millennium dawned, *Neighbors, a non-fiction investigation of the massacre* by Polish-born professor Jan Gross was published. Based on testimonials of Jews and Poles, it seemed to reveal the main parties involved in expediting the murder of Jewish residents in town were Polish. Some even from their community.

The discussions provoked by Neighbors sometimes took on a sharply polemical character, as reporters, intellectuals, and political figures, church representatives, and a range of others debated issues of real consequence to Polish self-understanding and self-esteem. The debate they launched was a serious one. It was also highly contentious, for it turned on vital questions of national history, character, culture, honor, guilt, innocence, responsibility, self-image, image abroad, and more. There were those who wrote out of anger and indignation, rejecting Gross's arguments outright and refusing any acknowledgment of Polish guilt or responsibility for wartime atrocities against Jews. Some were apologetic, admitting a degree of culpability but pointing to mitigating circumstances to explain the wartime killings of Jews. Disturbingly, earlier charges of zydokomuna, Jewish collusion with the communists were revived, leading to explanations that said in light of such treachery, the Jews of Poland only got what they deserved. At its farthest extreme, a kind of "Jedwabne denial" took hold and contributors to right-wing publications and Internet chat rooms commonly claimed that the whole Jedwabne matter was nothing but "Holocaust business," a plot by Jews to defame Poland and prepare the ground for massive restitution claims.

(*Facing Jedwabne* by Alvin H. Rosenfeld, AJC—Global Jewish Advocacy)

Soon after this revelation, the Polish president visited the town in 2001 and, in a ceremony of remembrance, changed the words on the plaque, explaining:

For this crime we should beg the souls of the dead and their families for forgiveness. This is why today, as a citizen and as the president of the Republic of Poland, I beg pardon. I beg pardon in my own name and in the name of those Poles whose conscience is shattered by that crime.

(President Kwasniewski—July 10, 2001)

Jedwabne, almost to a man, drew their curtains and closed their doors, unwilling to participate in their President's gesture toward the Jewish people. Even to this day, almost all the people of Jedwabne reject that explanation.

During my return to Poland in 2008, as I was still contemplating the whole vision of reconciliation, I was in the Jewish quarter of Krakow, browsing through some local Judaica shops. Periodically I would ask if the owners were actually Jewish. I found the reactions rather alarming. None were Jewish and they seemed surprised to even be asked such a question. Clearly some clerks found it distasteful that I might mistake them for being Jewish.

But one young woman took the opportunity of my query to speak her heart about the history of the Jews in her homeland. She had a deep love for the Jewish people and Israel, and felt her country had not been forthcoming in their part of what happened in the Holocaust and after. It was she who introduced me to the slim volume entitled *Neighbors*. She suggested I read it to better understand what was at stake. This was the little book that tore Poland's conscience apart when it was first published in 2000. The stark and graphic pages of that little paperback were my first introduction to Jedwabne.

A year or so later, following the success of our first adventure with *A Tour of Roses*, my new-found Polish friend, Magda, asked if I had ever heard of Jedwabne. My stomach immediately knotted up. It took almost a year to read all the pages of that little book I picked up in the bookstore in Krakow. For some reason, what happened there seemed so much more immediate and personal than the Nazis' premeditated, sterile final solution. It was more sudden and visceral, entirely without compassion. Magda explained she had met a young woman from that town and in the course of their conversation, Magda shared her feelings about Jewish people and how God had touched and healed her heart from anti-Semitism. The woman shook with fear and could hardly continue talking at that point. Sometime after that encounter, Magda asked if I would consider bringing *A Tour of Roses* to Jedwabne.

I remember discussing the situation with the senior pastor of our church, as well as another pastor who has been an ongoing mentor in my life. I even asked Dallas Willard, a well-known theologian who was part of our fellowship at the time. All of them, in different ways, warned me to be certain this was really God's leading. The whole idea of *A Tour of Roses* was still very young and green. We had experienced a real sense of accomplishment in our first endeavor, but each time we went out into new territory, places we had never been and were not even invited to go. I didn't want to include Jedwabne, yet I could not exorcise it from my head or heart. Despite all warnings it soon became clear the Lord was leading us there.

One of the most significant signs along the way was when a British couple who were prayer warriors in Krakow, Mark and Cathy Warwick, agreed to go scout out the town with Viola, a Polish friend of theirs who was also Jewish.

Viola told the Lord, "They have to repent before they can be forgiven."

But as she approached the Jewish memorial the Lord spoke to her heart, saying, *When they see My love they will repent.*

In 2010 we planned our outreach to include 1,000 roses for Nuremberg 1,000 roses for Krakow, and 350 of the sweetest smelling roses for Jedwabne. These were delivered to us in Warsaw a few hours before we set out on the road to Jedwabne. I personally cleaned each one, all the while wondering and praying about the people in the town. Placing the flowers in buckets and packing up the van we made our way, trusting the brisk British GPS voice to steer us through the lonely nocturnal countryside to a small inn just outside town.

The next morning after breakfast and devotions, as we got ready to go, the innkeeper expressed real fear at the idea of our team walking through Jedwabne to give away these roses. She was especially concerned for those of us who were Jewish.

Ironically, three members of our team were Catholic, and that had presented some personal challenges for me. I had not encountered many believing Catholics who loved the Lord and were committed to following Him. But my concerns were quickly overcome when we actually met. It was clear their hearts were tender toward God and the Jewish people.

After walking and praying through the main parts of town, we unloaded buckets of roses near the square in a park-like area in the center. Many shops huddled around the square and their owners stood in the doorways, casually looking in our direction. There was a tangible heaviness in the atmosphere that all of us could feel. Large numbers of ravens sat up in the trees overhead, creating such a racket that it was hard to hear. Many buildings were older, as if part of a *shtetl* (small Jewish village in Eastern Europe) from centuries ago. But all their color had faded, just like an old photograph.

I asked the Polish part of the team to translate and support those of us who were Jewish as we gave out roses in and around the square. I felt in this case it was particularly important for those of us who were Jewish to be the people who actually handed out the roses. The rest of the team was very understanding and supportive.

The first two women my friend Evi and I encountered greeted us with hugs and kisses as we handed each a rose, explaining we were Jews from America. We told them the rose was a gift, a way to share God's love with them. As we continued to hand out roses in the shops and around the square, some people took time to warm to the idea. Others were quiet and thoughtful. Many were amazed. Almost everyone read the card tied to each rose, with its short verse entitled, *A Rose of Remembrance.* One man asked why we were doing this and I responded because there comes a time to heal.

He said, "Why now?"

I said, "Why not? If not now, when?"

Marek, one of the Polish members of the team, accompanied me as I gave out roses in a little grocery store/coffee place. Everyone received them very passively, without comment, but immediately began reading the cards. Halfway down the street from the store, a young man ran after us to thank us deeply and profusely. It was a beautiful moment.

One of our team was the remarkable Leonid, who came to us on temporary "loan" from our friends at Jews for Jesus in the Ukraine. Leonid, with the help of two Polish co-workers, prayed with five or six people to receive the Lord that day.

As the roses circulated through Jedwabne it seemed like the trees, the shops, and the people—which had earlier appeared so grey, dreary, and suspicious—slowly filled up with fresh color; they somehow warmed, as if by soaking in the sun they had become more welcoming. Children perched on benches in the square with lovely red roses in their hands and many of the shopkeepers were holding our flowers and smiling. I wondered, as I often have since, can an entire town be changed by such a simple act of kindness? That night we celebrated the goodness of God.

The next afternoon we walked over to the Jewish memorial on the edge of town. The sky was heavy and dark, overcast with clouds with a chill wind. The stone for the memorial housed a charred piece of wood in its middle. It was a chunk of the actual barn where most of the Jews of Jedwabne, with their children, were burned alive.

Perhaps some people journey to a place like this only to visit the memorial and to remind themselves what happened some 70 years ago. Others may choose to minister to the residents of the town, having nothing to do with the memorial since that is the past. In my opinion, the first choice misses the opportunity to connect with some good people who live and work in this town, who may be hungry for God, longing for His mercy and grace in their lives. They may not have answers for what happened all those years ago, but they deeply desire healing. The second group may not want to connect to the history of the town at all, which still affects this community today. The euphoria of reaching souls for the Lord and sharing His love is powerful indeed. We experienced both parts of the whole, and I believe there is a balance to the picture that the Lord would have us see.

It was hard standing there, facing the wood and stone, none of us indifferent to the silent but powerful witness of man's depravity. The words on the memorial now read:

TO THE MEMORY OF JEWS FROM YEDWABNE AND THE SURROUNDING AREA,
MEN, WOMEN, AND CHILDREN, CO-INHABITANTS OF THIS LAND, WHO WERE
MURDERED AND BURNED ALIVE ON THIS SPOT ON JULY 10, 1941.

It was painful for those of us who were Jewish and those of us who were Polish. Time ceased as we grieved, prayed, and worshiped the Lord. Confessing and declaring His goodness, we ultimately pronounced God's blessing over the community from that forlorn place. I can still see Kasia as she knelt in the weeds, interceding for both our people. It took our British friend, Mark, to hear what the Lord required in that moment. *If you can stand in this place and forgive the town, then God will move and bring healing.*

There were five of us on the team that year who were Jewish by birth. All of us had been rejoicing the night before, amazed at the incredible victory God gave us as we shared the roses and His love with the people in town. But this was a completely different moment. Each of us profoundly sobered by the realization of what had happened in this community clearly heard Mark call us to forgive. We stood together on the crest overlooking the town, with the memorial in front of us, silently wrestling with feelings we were experiencing in that moment. Finally, I asked Leonid to recite the Aaronic benediction in Hebrew over the town for us—to bless them as we have been unconditionally blessed over the centuries by the eternal words God appointed Aaron to speak over the children of Israel.

The Lord bless you and keep you;
The Lord make His face shine upon you,
And be gracious to you;
The Lord lift up His countenance upon you,
And give you peace.
(Numbers 6:24-26)

Dear People of Jedwabne,

My name is Olivier Melnick, I am a Jew who was born in Paris, France and now lives in the USA. I lost my grandfather in Auschwitz and this could make me very bitter and angry.

But in 1983, I found what I was not looking for and I have never been the same since. I found my Messiah and Savior in the person of Yeshua HaMashiach.

My prayer for you is this: May the God of the universe who controls all things, pour out His love on you and may His Spirit touch you and change you like He changed me 28 years ago. The world is full of hatred, deceit and violence as it rejects the Savior Yeshua (Jesus). Only through Him and His death and resurrection can we be forgiven and loved so much so that we can also extend Messiah's love to others. Messiah loved me enough to die for me, He loves you enough that He also died for you. Trust him for your life and share His love and His shalom with others.

In Yeshua's Love,

Olivier

(Olivier Melnick, Chosen People Ministries, from the collection of prayers and blessings for Jedwabne)

10

JEDWABNE REVISITED

We returned to Jedwabne in 2012. As we prepared to go I prayed about what we might offer to the people of the town, if anything. The single idea the Lord gave me was to collect prayers of blessing from people in Messianic congregations everywhere I toured during the eight months prior to the actual project. Magda's co-worker translated all the prayers into Polish, and Heatherly artfully arranged them together in a beautiful rose scrapbook we found the very first Sunday in Warsaw. We planned to present it to the priests the following Sunday, sometime after the Mass. But we also took seven prayers and printed them up on 4 different prayer cards. English on one side, Polish on the other. We made a hundred of each of those cards. I encouraged the team to hand them out only as they felt led by the Spirit to do so.

We walked through the town, praying, and I saw this man looking at us from across the street. His was the only family (that we know of) to shelter a little Jewish girl. Even her sister was killed. The man started telling his story as soon as we gave him a prayer card. And he said it was the Germans who forced them at gunpoint to do the terrible things they did. The man needed to tell his story. But at a certain point we stopped him. I began to realize at that moment, it wasn't for us to know who did it. In a sense, that didn't matter so much anymore. What mattered was the loss that happened and the grieving that needs to come so that healing may follow. There may very well be those who need to acknowledge/confess their sins. And maybe all need to deal with their feelings of fear or indifference to what happened, their hardness of heart, but only God can bring them that revelation, and it doesn't come with a voice of condemnation, but the invitation that Love brings, to be free of our sin through repentance...

(Sally Klein O'Connor—Journal Entry—June 19, 2012)

That Sunday we awoke early to attend the middle service for the Mass in town. It was packed. I had no idea there were so many people living there. There were no unoccupied seats so we stood with many others. At one point we knelt, with everyone else, for at least 20 minutes. The floor was marble—cold and hard. But it was there, on my knees praying, the Lord spoke a word to my heart for those gathered.

I am here in this place reaching for these people but they don't see Me. They only see the priest, but I am beyond him, reaching for My children, and reaching for him (the priest) also. I see him as a Father sees a son. Healing will come to this city and to the priests. I will open the hearts of this people and rain down upon them My mercies, which are new every morning, for surely I am here in this place among them.

After the service, we were invited back for tea with the senior priest. But Sam and Gayle found themselves embroiled in a difficult exchange with a woman from the town. Deported to Siberia at just 6 months old, she survived the ordeal but held onto her anger over the years. She felt certain people owed the town of Jedwabne an apology because of all that happened. Per our first visit, I knew some residents felt the Jews in the community were in some way responsible for Polish people being sent to Siberia, many of whom never returned. But it had also been eventually revealed that both Poles and Jews exposed some of their neighbors who were then deported.

Sam finally extricated himself, but Gayle continued patiently listening to this woman vent her feelings in Polish until Heatherly managed to communicate to the woman that Gayle didn't understand a word of Polish. Gayle's philosophy was simple; "Sometimes people need to talk." It didn't matter to Gayle that he couldn't understand her words. He saw her need to vent her feelings and be heard.

The senior priest and two younger priests were even more warm and welcoming than the first time. I was able to share what I felt the Lord impressed on my heart during the service and the senior priest confirmed it. Gayle also had a word he felt led to share, and it was also received very graciously. But the priest, like the townspeople, made sure to explain how the Poles in town were not responsible for the horrible things Jan Gross wrote about in his book.

"You know they didn't do it," he reiterated.

"I wasn't there and you weren't there when it happened," I responded. "Even Jan Gross wasn't there when it happened. So, none of us can know for sure. But God knows. He even knows what was in the hearts of all those who were there and witnessed what happened."

The priest emphasized several inaccuracies in the book, but this time he also added that some things were true.

I saw his position much more clearly than I did in 2010. He needed to advocate for the people in his parish. While we were not necessarily agreed about what happened in the 1941 massacre, both the priest and I concurred that the people of Jedwabne were in need of deep healing.

We presented him with the scrapbook before the middle Mass and he leafed through some pages. A few of the prayers bothered him because they were in response to our understanding the Poles had participated in the massacre, so there was a lot about God's forgiveness. He felt some of those petitions might be hurtful. But others were very beautiful, and he said he would share them with the parish.

He surprised me several times as we dialogued with the help of Bibi, one of our interpreters. He talked about how he sent his associates to Alpha Training, a Protestant outreach through hospitality and discussion, hoping they could eventually begin small groups in

Jedwabne. I thought my jaw would fall off my face, considering the Alpha course is very evangelistic. He continued, saying he believed there is one flock and one shepherd and the Messianic Jewish movement is a forerunner of what's to come. I was pretty amazed these ideas were being spoken in this town, of all places, and by a Catholic priest!

There was one more item I felt compelled to share, that some healing might come to Jedwabne if the people were ever willing to join us at the Jewish memorial on the edge of town and say Kaddish (the Jewish prayer of blessing recited when people have died). The priest couldn't imagine how it might happen. "That would be very hard." It didn't surprise me. *I* found it difficult to imagine. We ended by praying for the priest and the town. I was very encouraged by his genuinely warm and honest reception.

The final thing we did before leaving town was pray and worship at the Jewish Memorial. I took out my keyboard and began singing and praying. Sam walked over to the Jewish cemetery across the road and worshiped with his guitar.

At one point I happened to look up the road and saw someone walking toward us. Instantly my heart jumped in my chest and I thought, *This is it—this is a seed.* I felt like a little child watching God do the beautiful and impossible thing.

Marek, a town resident, wandered over to where we were. We had met in the square the day before, when I was singing, and Bibi, Heatherly, and I had prayed for him. His father was an alcoholic who beat him so badly his right eye couldn't close properly, and his speaking was slow. His father died some years before, and Marek grew up hating all the alcoholics in town. There were quite a few. I asked Sam to lead us in saying the Kaddish. Marek was more than willing to participate.

Once again, I saw the hand of the Lord working in hidden ways, where no one would think to look—in a tiny town, in front of a weed-infested memorial—remembering His people. I saw His sovereign goodness on display, at work to redeem. To Him belongs all glory and praise!

"The voice of the man I love! Here he comes, bounding over the mountains, skipping over the hills! My darling is like a gazelle or young stag. There he is, standing outside our wall, looking in through the windows, peering in through the lattice. My darling speaks; he is saying to me, 'Get up, my love! My beauty! Come away! For you see that the winter has passed, the rain is finished and gone, the flowers are appearing in the countryside, the time has come for [the birds] to sing, and the cooing of doves can be heard in the land. The fig trees are forming their unripe figs, and the grapevines in bloom give out their perfume. Get up, my love, my beauty! Come away!'"

(Song of Songs 2:8-13)

As we come out of the winter, Lord, and into the spring, we are reminded of how you can bring life from what was once dead. How a tree loses all its leaves in the fall and looks dead all winter. In the winter nothing grows there are no flowers and there is no beauty. But as the seasons change and the cold days disappear and the warmth of the sun returns, we see how life once again blossoms.

I ask Yeshua, my King, that the time of winter be over for these people. I ask that You bring the rain of new life washing away the old life and once again bring Your healing water. As the flowers come up from seeds that were planted long ago, I ask You, Yeshua, to water the seeds of healing to these people of Jedwabne. Let the seeds of life in You grow strong and deep. Let the words of truth be known in each and every household in this land. Light the way of Your word over each father. As we need the sun to bring the light for the plants to grow. Let the light of the true Son shine on father, mother, sons and daughters that they may know of Your love and forgiveness.

Sally Klein O'Connor

In the service of Messiah,

Messianic Rabbi Andrew Dinnerman

New Jersey

(From the collection of prayers and blessings for Jedwabne)

70

11

A CONSPIRACY OF KINDNESS

"Kindness has converted more sinners than zeal, eloquence, or learning."

Frederick W. Faber

So much of the journey with *A Tour of Roses* is really about obedience. It's not necessarily what I want to do, or what I think may be a good idea. It's what I believe comes to me from God through prayer, reading the Bible, and revelation. I believe God still communicates actively with His creation. He loves us, has not ever stopped loving us, and therefore wants relationship with us—deep and personal. Like a lover, or true friend who cares about the unseen places in our hearts, God is gentle but persistent in searching us out through the Holy Spirit. Never in any farthest corner of my imagination did I perceive God steering me toward a project like *A Tour of Roses*, but it is clear now that He was. And every tool and turn in my life God has caused to serve a much larger purpose than I can grasp, even now.

When pondering the whole attitude I grew up with in regard to the Holocaust, I see now that my understanding was still so small and narrow. I was sure He must want me to minister in some way to Germany, and I thought, *I could spend my life ministering in all the corners of Germany the vast mercy and grace of my Lord.* But, as with many things in life, my vision was too small. I still remember a dear friend, Rabbi

Barry Budoff, saying, "It's bigger than you know." To me, it was already huge.

Preparing to go to Germany for the first time in 2007, I remember telling a long-time Calvary Chapel pastor all the ideas that were in my heart about how I might minister the love and mercy of God in Germany as a Jew. The afternoon softly shifted into twilight as we stood and talked. He said quietly, "This is from God." I quivered a little inside. I knew it was so. But still, when someone speaks with that much conviction what you already believe to be true, it becomes inescapable.

He continued, "You need to go to Auschwitz."

"No I don't. It's all about Germany," I responded, confident I had a grip on what God was doing.

"Pray about it. You really should go to Auschwitz…"

From the very beginning it was larger than Germany. To this day, it continues expanding in many ways. There are moments when God sets before us an opportunity to participate in something He is already doing, but because of our wounded perspective it appears utterly impossible.

Some years ago I attended a Vineyard conference in Anaheim focused around *Conspiracy of Kindness*—an idea birthed by Steve Sjogren. I was immediately interested. Here was something different, giving into the community with no strings attached to demonstrate the unconditional love of God. Pretty awesome! And it was.

There was a worship band outreach that afternoon and I accompanied them, singing on the summer streets of Anaheim, handing out ice cold bottles of water to shop owners and people walking in the heat of the day. It was sweet—very freeing—and as I walked with them, an idea stirred. How would it be if I sang about the unconditional love of God in front of an abortion clinic? No obligatory pictures, no efforts to stop women who had an appointment—no rhetoric at all. Just sweet songs about the mercy and love of God that flows from His throne to all who have eyes to see and ears to hear.

After all, wasn't that what His Kingdom was all about? Expressing the unconditional love of God in dark places of bondage? I was hooked. As it happens, I had been on both sides of this issue long before I came to faith. I experienced an abortion while in college, though no embryo was found. And later, pregnant again, I carried my little girl the whole way, releasing her to parents who would care for her better than I was able to at that time in my life.

I spent a few days praying and writing out a whole plan, expecting several people to participate from my church. But that was not the case.

At first the leadership didn't understand why I felt the need to bring worship to an abortion clinic. Why not do it on the street—or at a gas station like the team in Anaheim did? I only knew the idea kept pressing into me despite other people's uncertainty. I didn't even know what the plan was—just that God was clearly speaking to step out. I wondered if I might be a little crazy, even as I felt so euphoric. My pastor counseled me to start a small home group in preparation for this little "mission." We met together for several weeks as God readied our hearts, some of us to intercede in prayer, and one or two of us to actually stand and worship. Soon the day arrived—God spoke clearly through a message our pastor gave that it was time.

I will always remember walking down to a very visible corner in my neighborhood, where a particular clinic had stood for some 30 years. Carrying my keyboard, wondering what would happen as soft words rose questioning my intent. *What's the big deal? Why are you making such a fuss? There's nothing happening here, in the middle of the day. What is it you think you are going to do?*

I had no idea what would be accomplished. I was only following. For a moment it all loomed up before me so big and impossible—*and unnecessary*, whispered the voice—and almost cartoonish, that I should set my keyboard down in the planter at the edge of the parking lot facing the clinic. But I did it anyway. I turned on my keyboard, opened my mouth and sang. People listened. Even the doctors and staff stood at the far end smoking, staring, and listening. I showed up almost every

Friday after that, whenever I was in town, for nearly a year. I witnessed the pain and shame on the faces of many women who walked in, and sometime later walked out. For those who changed their minds and those who went through with it, for the doctors and nurses, and boyfriends way too eager to drop off their girlfriends, I sang and sang about the unending love of God and His incredible mercy. Some women who were in tears received prayer from my friends before or after the procedure, and even literature on alternatives. I believe a few may have chosen differently because we stood in that place, worshiping and praying.

Five years later, the clinic disappeared altogether. I can't help wondering if all our worship and prayers in that place had something to do with shutting it down. A dental office took its place along with a kosher pizza joint. Years later our middle daughter, Bonnie, worked for the dentist for a season. Nothing lasts forever.

"The grass withers and the flower fades, but the word of our God stands forever." (Isaiah 40:8)

In the moment God sets before us a particular opportunity to join Him in something He is doing, it's hard to know what the outcome will be. And that is certainly a large part of how we are taught to make decisions in this world—weighing out the pros and cons of participating.

We may not even understand, at the beginning, why God is calling us to this particular person, place, or thing. And this also creates difficulty for us. I know it does for me. I want to understand what we are doing and why. In some small way I feel a little more in control when I understand the situation. But I have found quite often God isn't looking to soothe our souls in this way. He is challenging us to trust Him.

With God the question is always one of obedience. Will we do it or not? Will Peter step out on the water and discover a miracle? Will Moses lead the Israelites out of bondage? Will Esther go before the king? When we understand that it is God who is inviting us to join Him in what He is already doing, how will we respond? The issue at stake is *always* our obedience, which is the real evidence of our love for Him. It is never about the outcome. That belongs to God.

I still remember setting up my keyboard for the first time in 2009, along the dirt walkway where prisoners were marched to the gas chambers in Auschwitz-Birkenau. In my mind it was an impossible thing that we should gather like this publicly, in such a place as Birkenau, to worship. The same kind of whispers I heard on the first day I stood and sang at the abortion clinic seemed to materialize from nowhere. But as the team gathered around me, sitting and standing and we began to worship, the impossible became possible—even glorious.

12

LOVE NEVER FAILS

"For He Himself is our peace, who has made the two groups one and has destroyed the barrier, the dividing wall of hostility, by setting aside in His flesh the law with its commands and regulations. His purpose was to create in Himself one new humanity out of the two, thus making peace, and in one body to reconcile both of them to God through the cross, by which He put to death their hostility. He came and preached peace to you who were far away and peace to those who were near. For through Him we both have access to the Father by one Spirit."

(Ephesians 2:14-18)

"And now these three remain: faith, hope and love. But the greatest of these is love."

(1 Corinthians 13:13)

Perhaps the most basic theology for *A Tour of Roses* is best summed up in these three words: Love never fails. I believe with all my heart this is absolute truth. When we choose to love others as Jesus loves us, that love will not fail. It doesn't matter what it looks like to everyone else—or even to us—or how long it takes. God will make good on His word because He is faithful.

At the same time, it is an impossible word in a troubled time in our nation and in our world today. Everywhere you turn, love is a rare commodity, at least the kind Paul is speaking about. Just as we have learned to make things that no longer last a lifetime—things with planned obsolescence—it seems we have done the same with marriage. We fall out of love almost as easily as we fall in, and sacrifice is something that rarely crosses the mind of this generation. The love Paul speaks about is completely foreign to us, but is demonstrated by Jesus as he washes the feet of Judas, knowing he will betray Him. Choosing—even in that circumstance—to love.

When I was a child, my little brother, Michael, and I were often at odds. Sometime, early on, Michael decided lying was easier than facing unpleasant consequences. Ever fearful he would end up in bigger trouble than he could handle, I would always beg him to "fess up," hoping someone besides myself would be able to talk him out of his bad ideas. My brother never appreciated my point of view.

Even when there were painful consequences, I felt telling the truth was the right thing to do. I never questioned that premise. It was etched into my soul.

Looking back, I think what my brother truly needed was love. That greater love which also embraces truth, but not the taskmaster I served. I realize now that truth—as I thought about it then—was a relentless, unforgiving standard that had to be maintained at the cost of almost everything else. The fact that I couldn't live up to my own ideal of it should have given me a clue that maybe truth wasn't quite the way I perceived it.

I see now that truth without love often becomes our reason for what we like to call justice. But God's justice is so much larger and deeper than the mere assembling of facts in some kind of chronological order and often-accusatory style. God's justice is steeped in unconditional love for people who don't care, who spit and curse, who wound, abandon, and may even kill us. The love we receive from the Lord and are called to participate in lives for an audience of One, unafraid and unashamed to be an instrument in our Father's redemptive plan.

Of course, I am not speaking of earthly affections. I am referring to the heavenly empowerment of the Holy Spirit at work in us, "… Christ in you, the hope of glory." (Colossians 1:27) To the degree we are willing to allow the Lord's love to consume our small, frail, petty attractions is the degree in which we truly participate in the Kingdom of God at work in and around us. It is, quite honestly, a losing of ourselves and this is what we fear most. But the result can only be gain.

I often think of the story of *The Velveteen Rabbit*. We come into this life all shiny, new, and innocent—or so it seems. And then life happens. Over time, the plush parts of our bodies and souls are rubbed raw and worn down as we realize we are losing our life as we have known it. But for those who open their hearts up to Jesus, there is another process going on. All the selfishness and dross is being burned up and off as the pure flow of God's love is ever increasing in our souls and we continue to work out our salvation in fear and trembling. Pretty soon all that superficial beauty is gone and the deeper, eternal glory of an unfading soul emerges in its place as we become more real—more alive and free—than we ever were when we clung to our initial shininess and lived in the shallows.

We are not absent in this process. It is not as though the Lord sets us aside while He works through us, despite us. We do not channel the Holy Spirit. It is a partnership, through our willingness, and worship, and our surrender. It is a conscious choice to love with His love.

In 1999 both my parents passed away. Both had given me power of attorney. Dad and I had built a real foundation of trust over the last few years of his life. Even when he struggled with dementia and the early stages of Alzheimer's, he trusted enough to listen and let me help him navigate through his confusion.

But when Mom was in the hospital, fighting to live, there was a turning point when she decided I was only there to help her because of the money. All her anger and bitterness surfaced and all her love and favor, which I had known for most of my life, evaporated. I had spent most of my years trying to please and honor her, attempting to make up for all the loss in her life. She was the person I most admired and loved. But it wasn't until she withdrew her affection that I had the greatest opportunity to love her truly, without expectation of anything in return.

I felt the Lord speak to my heart: *It's been easy to love her most of your life because you have always known that she loved you. But now you have the opportunity to love her unconditionally, the way I love you.*

Toward the end of her time in the hospital the nurses were not changing her bedclothes as often, or her diaper. She was very raw. At first, I didn't know what to do about it. She was so angry with me—with them—with everyone and everything. She didn't want me to do anything for her, but she was also in pain and needed some help.

Finally, I told her, "While you are living, we are going to do the things that are about living." And I cleaned her up as gently and thoroughly as I could, even as she vented at me.

In all the time I spoke and sang about Jesus to my mom, it was only in that too short season that I actually *gave* her Christ through my choice to love unconditionally in the face of her rancor and rage.

When I traveled to Germany and Poland in 2007 it was an eye-opening experience! To recognize there were real wounds among the people of Germany and Poland—deep wells of shame and condemnation—was a revelation. Before God's intervention, I had never given a single thought as to whether the Germans struggled with what happened in the Holocaust. All I knew was the constant pain on the Jewish front. Because this grief was without end, there could never be any forgiveness, and therefore the Germans would not ever experience release or closure. As Israeli President, Reuven Rivlin recently tweeted (April 2019) in response to Brazilian President Jair's comment that the crimes of the Holocaust can be forgiven, "… We will never forgive and never forget. No one will order the forgiveness of the Jewish people, and it can never be bought in the name of interests."

Nothing has released Germany from their shame. Not great sums of money, or sincere public expressions of regret, not personal apology, nor the many memorials Germany has built or preserved in remembrance of the Shoah. So while the Germans have rebuilt their country and economy, their hearts have never been restored.

As I have shared these observations with Jewish friends, believers and non-believers, I have seen three main reactions. The first is anger. This comes from people who don't buy anything German and teach their children to do the same through the generations. The Germans are not ever to be trusted according to this group of people.

The second group still grieves and remains paralyzed by the depth and breadth of the *Shoah*. They cannot conceive how God will ever bind up this abyss of sorrow.

Lastly, there are those few, whom I now gladly count myself among, that have just begun to see God's heart on this issue. He wants to bring wholeness between Jews and Germans, cleansing the Germans from their shame and condemnation, and freeing the Jews from judgment and unforgiveness.

We who have experienced the forgiveness of God through His Son's sacrifice know that He calls murderers, thieves, and whores to become His daughters and sons and to represent the Kingdom of God on Earth. We stand delivered from the heavy yoke of shame and condemnation, and are exhorted—even admonished—to forgive as we have been forgiven. We know nothing good lives in us, apart from Him who poured His life into us. Therefore, we judge no man according to the flesh. We are learning to look with the eyes of God and to see with His heart.

There is a deep hunger and thirst for healing among the peoples of Germany and Poland—and for the forgiveness only Messiah can bring. As Isaiah declared, "How beautiful on the mountains are the feet of those who bring good news..." Does it not sound like God's good pleasure to use the children of the Holocaust generation to minister the Lord's healing, mercy, and forgiveness to those who bear the legacy of the perpetrators of this evil? This does not mean we should ignore the sins of the past. But, perhaps, there is a less alienating way to make sure something like this will happen Never Again. My hope is that we can find a redemptive way to remember with our German brothers and sisters in the Lord that will bear witness to the world of the Love of Messiah.

And isn't that the work we are supposed to be about?

13

A SIGN AND A WONDER

"... and live a life of love, just as Christ loved us and gave Himself for us as a fragrant offering and sacrifice to God."

(Ephesians 5:2)

My husband, Michael, and I attend the Valley Vineyard Christian Fellowship in Reseda, California and have been involved in this fellowship for over 30 years. In that time we have seen some amazing moves of God. Signs and wonders, along with worship, are among the key values of Vineyard churches. Our fellowship embraces all the gifts of the Spirit, but healing is a core value. Whether it's an instantaneous physical healing everyone can bear witness to or the moment-by-moment healing of emotionally shattered people becoming more whole, both are miraculous. Both are the result of Love.

As human beings we search for what we can hear with our ears, see with our eyes, and touch with our hands. Disney, Harry Potter, and many other books and movie characters give us an appetite for magic. Magic is about power, but miracles are about love. They are the expression of a heavenly Father's passion for His children. That same love is then transmitted through us to the world. Many speculate as to why we don't see more signs and wonders in the American church. But

82

I believe Love is the sign and wonder God is looking to express first and foremost in and through His Body today.

In September 2010 we embarked on a second outreach in Europe for *A Tour of Roses*. Each of us had a unique opportunity to express the love of God through worship and acts of kindness. Toward the end of a concert at Sala Jakuba, a one-thousand-year-old Franciscan monastery in Krakow, Poland, I found myself saying, "We came to love you." It just fell out of my mouth. I questioned myself later. Is that really accurate? In retrospect I realize that's exactly what we came to do.

That's the mission, that's the calling: To love! But most of us would rather do anything else. I can freely offer up my day, my life, my voice, my time, my knowledge, my talent, my body for the sake of the Gospel and still find myself clutching my heart and standing outside that offering. In other words, I can give everything to God and still not actually willingly surrender myself to Him.

I was convicted on that same trip when team members, Heatherly and Marek, spent the better part of an hour talking to an old Polish man in the memorial square for the Krakow Jewish ghetto. He was five years old when he saw bodies of Jewish adults and children stacked up in the square. The memory seared his soul and he stopped believing in God. He was afraid for Heatherly because she is Jewish and said how dangerous it was for us to be in this place because of the strong anti-Semitism. He couldn't wrap his mind around why we would come there and give out roses. Heatherly was able to give him a CD, but he told her he would not attend the concert. Afterwards, Heatherly was crying over this old Polish man, his pain, and his inability to believe in a merciful God. She fearlessly extended her heart in the flood of God's love to him and could not remain untouched by his pain in the process.

Sometimes we don't want to actually engage with our hearts when we share the Good News. Some of us may be thinking more along these lines, "Jesus loves you. Don't shoot the messenger." But Jesus wept as He looked over Jerusalem and saw the future. His heart loved the rich young ruler who couldn't give up his earthly treasure so that he could store up treasure in heaven. He was deeply grieved at the grave of Lazarus. And how hard was it for Him to care for and serve Judas and Peter, knowing each would betray Him? I think sometimes we want to dispense the Gospel while wearing a surgical mask and latex gloves, so we can protect ourselves from the very people we are ministering to. Sterile is not the same as holy. Nothing grows in a sterile environment—not bacteria and not roses.

During our first trip for *A Tour of Roses* in 2009, we reached out to the community of Bergen. We handed out roses and I did a concert in the park that night. Afterward, the whole team was invited to the organizer's home to share supper with her family and friends. As my friend, Dagmar, pointed out, this was not something usually done with outsiders. We sat at Katharina's supper table with her friends and family. Most were not believers, yet they expressed a real appreciation that we reached out to them in love.

But the following day we visited the former concentration camp, Bergen-Belsen, and for some on my team it was the hardest thing we did. Each memorial stone stood for a mass grave of Jews mostly, who were murdered in that place. Suddenly the warmth and wonder of what happened just 24 hours before with the people of the town seemed a billion miles away as we walked through the markers of the Holocaust in that unnaturally still and silent place.

I have come to realize both things are true. We need the courage to look at each and engage. Sometimes we forgive on a superficial level because we know forgiveness is essential in our walk with the Lord. And we don't want to think too deeply about the actual issue lest it become a stumbling block in our ability to forgive. But if we understand what Jesus did on the cross, there is nothing we cannot forgive. It's a matter of taking hold of His grace while looking at the object of our pain, understanding and believing that His blood is enough. Because it is.

At the end of the concert at Sala Jakuba, I invited the crowd to come up front, lay down their unforgiveness, bitterness, and judgment, and take up the love of God as they picked a rose from the bucket. One woman got up a minute or two after I resumed singing. Then streams of people walked to the front and took roses for themselves. A man who had been identified as someone with deep anti-Semitic feelings was the second person to come up and take a rose.

And yet it's not enough to stop hating, or even to forgive. What is needed is a willingness to love. If Jesus lives in us then the capacity to love even our enemies resides in us because He, whose very nature is love, abides in us.

How do we connect to that love? I think it happens when we choose to be present, to be fully alive to God, to ourselves, and to each other. To engage. And it *is* a scary thing. It means we are vulnerable to rejection and all kinds of other issues we struggle with and the other person may struggle with. This doesn't even include the kind of painful history on a national level we encountered during A Tour of Roses. But it is, perhaps, the most magnificent quality of human beings: that we can choose to love as God has loved us—unconditionally. In this, we most reflect our Creator.

The *free love* of the 60s and the *tolerance* of our time are pale shadows, deceits, and counterfeits of this reality. The real thing is so powerful and deep we don't have adequate words to express its height, depth, and breadth. The incarnation of that love was seen, heard, and touched once upon a time in the person of Jesus of Nazareth.

It is my personal prayer to live and breathe that love more and more. My great hope is when people encounter those of us who call ourselves His disciples, His love would be evident in every area of our lives to such a degree that people would feel about us as John felt about Jesus. When they hear, see, or touch us, it will be as though they have encountered that which John spoke of—the very incarnation of Love alive in us.

"That which was from the beginning, which we have heard, which we have seen with our eyes, which we have looked at and our hands have touched—this we proclaim concerning the Word of life. The life appeared; we have seen it and testify to it, and we proclaim to you the eternal life, which was with the Father and has appeared to us. We proclaim to you what we have seen and heard, so that you also may have fellowship with us. And our fellowship is with the Father and with his Son, Jesus Christ. We write this to make our joy complete."

(1 John 1:1-4)

14

FORGIVING AND LOVING OUR ENEMIES

"The truth of the matter is: Very ordinary people do extraordinary evil. We need to judge them, surely, and forgive them, if we can, because they are responsible.

And because we need to be healed.

If forgiving is a remedy for the wounds of a painful past, we cannot deny any human being the possibility of being forgiven lest we deny the victim the possibility of being healed through forgiving."

(Forgive and Forget: Healing the Hurts We Don't Deserve by Lewis B. Smedes*)*

"Father, forgive them, for they do not know what they are doing."

(Luke 23:34)

From the very beginning of our ministry, I felt the Lord impress on me that our walk with Him is determined by the way we see God, ourselves, and others. I started out with very negative views about myself and great uncertainty about whether God could use someone as messed up as me. My view of other people was also colored by all the broken places in my heart and mind. Quite often my default position was defensive and judgmental. But somehow, in the grace of God, there was freedom to sing and minister from His heart. When I would minister in a flow of His love and grace I saw things very differently than I did most of the time.

But often I would return to my default-operating mode before we drove out of the church parking lot. It took a long time for me to realize God wanted to change *me*—not the ministry.

Taught how to think about Germany through the lens of the Jewish culture, it never occurred to me there might be another view that actually represented the heart of God. I believed my thoughts and feelings about what happened in the Holocaust to be completely valid and unquestionably justified. I had no reason to think otherwise until the Lord revealed His point of view in this matter.

As a result we began *A Tour of Roses*. From the start I felt strongly it was not my place to forgive. My understanding originated from a fundamental Jewish ideology, which asserts we can only pardon people for those things directly done to us. In other words, we don't have a right to forgive what was perpetrated on others, even if they are our people. This especially relates to issues concerning the Holocaust.

As a good friend who is also a Messianic rabbi wrote me in response to my questions about forgiving the Germans and Poles:

> The Germans and the Poles are not my enemies, so I cannot forgive them for myself. Nor can I forgive them for God. Nor should I forgive them for others who hold things against them. I can sympathize with them, just as I could sympathize with any other suffering person. But again, they are not my enemies, so how can I forgive them?

> I recognize your sense of call. I affirm and respect your compassion for Poles or Germans who live under a pall of guilt. However I am not at all comfortable with representing the Jewish people as an agent of forgiveness. I believe it presumptuous and unintentionally disrespectful to those

whose lives have been lost or deeply touched by the Shoah (Holocaust), I believe it wiser for ME to tread carefully in this area. And remember that God does visit the iniquity of the fathers unto the children to the third and fourth generation. The pall that lies over Poland and Germany in this regard may be an expression of that truth. No, the current generation doesn't "deserve" it, but there were horrendous spiritual consequences of what the Third Reich did.

Initially I agreed with this point of view and wanted to tread carefully. So, I focused on loving and blessing the Germans and Poles as we handed out roses.

Up to a certain point I did not think about *A Tour of Roses* directly in regard to forgiveness. I thought of myself, and the people who participated in *A Tour of Roses*, as ambassadors of reconciliation according to what Paul says in 2 Corinthians 5:20. Furthermore, I thought of us as people desiring to express the extravagant love of God in a tangible way by handing out beautiful red roses.

But as I continued to minister abroad, particularly in Germany, I observed a society still wounded in their collective *soul* through their fathers' and grandfathers' choices in the Holocaust. While Germany is well put together on the outside, they're still riven at the core. To my knowledge there has never been any closure, forgiveness, or process for the Germans to work through psychologically or spiritually. No help was proffered which might have enabled them to come to terms with what happened to them as individuals and a nation under Hitler. Instead, what endures is indictment, accusation, guilt, condemnation, shame, suspicion, and unrelenting judgment, especially from the Jewish population. It's true there is some denial from the older generation. There is also resentment from the younger generation that there is no end to this legacy of shame and guilt they seem required to pass down. But it's important to recognize there are many who feel deep remorse for what happened in their families and nation.

Of course, the Jewish people are also profoundly wounded. But in our sorrow, we may fail to see and validate others who also suffer, especially those we once labeled enemies. Apart from Messiah, we might view their pain as some kind of justice. But when we elect to follow the Lord there is a higher call and a larger picture to consider. As Jews we may yearn for justice and retribution—an eye for an eye—but in Yeshua we are required to forgive, to bless and not curse. The traditional Jewish community continues to build museums and memorials to remind everyone what happened in the Holocaust must happen *Never Again.* But the ongoing corollary to the creation of these museums and memorials reminds the world of the terrible evils Germany and its allies perpetrated in the Holocaust.

If the intent in raising up all the museums and memorials of the Shoah is to be a reminder of what occurred in the hope of stopping genocide from ever happening again, it doesn't appear to have been successful. It seems to be in the very nature of mankind to choose badly, because sin is inherent in people.

We can never achieve true justice on this earth because we are crippled by the legacy of Adam and Eve. Only in the presence of God will justice and mercy be truly satisfied. Still, that doesn't mean we shouldn't attempt "to act justly and to love mercy and to walk humbly with your God." (Micah 6:8) But because we, as a people have identified so deeply with the issues of the Shoah, it seems that no amount of reparation and repentance on the part of Germany will heal our wound. In some cases our pain on this subject is an endless abyss, justified anew with every fresh discovery of evil during that season.

The problem is we don't think about if there is damage *we* may have caused by denying them some kind of closure. Instead, they are left with a hurt that never completely heals, and is constantly reopened so the world can remember.

Sometime ago I watched a documentary called *Hitler's Children* (made in 2011). It gave a brief portrait of some of the family of former Nazi officers. I will never forget the first segment. It was about Hermann Goering's grandniece. It showed her living in the desert with her husband. They had a few friends, but enjoyed their solitude. They never had children because she and her brother voluntarily sterilized themselves so Goering's line would not continue through them. I was shocked and could not imagine willingly making such a choice.

God has a much better plan. His desire is to redeem, not to destroy, and to change the very chemistry of the German people through the blood of His Son. I have seen the humility of Messiah expressed in some of my German friends. It is amazing to behold. Beautiful and powerful is their meekness in Him, the Lord of Hosts.

During the spring of 2014, *A Tour of Roses* project visited Mauthausen in Austria. We were immediately welcomed into a beautiful place with gardens and amazing hospitality. And it was there—in Mauthausen—that one of the most transcendent moments of the entire project occurred in a very unexpected place—within the formidable stone structure of a former concentration camp.

At a house concert I extended an invitation to everyone, asking them to join us for a time of worship the next morning at the camp. To my great surprise several people showed up. We gathered together in an outside area where plaques from many different nations were posted on the walls from various people groups who suffered within those austere confines. I pulled out my keyboard and we began to worship in Hebrew and English. My friends, Heatherly and Sam, who are Jewish believers, got up and danced together in a Messianic expression of worship on the cold stone pavement.

In a pause between songs the Austrians raised their voices in German, singing rich harmonies in major keys of faith, hope, and love. As they worshiped, I wept. The sky, which had been overcast and grey until then, began to clear as the clouds broke apart and the sun appeared. Who could imagine we would sit and stand, side by side in this place, raising our voices to God in major and minor keys, in Hebrew, German, and English? We gave God praise, honor, and glory on the very same stones where once we faced each other as enemies. We all stood in awe.

While there, we also visited a retirement home. Originally, we were denied access because of some genuine concern for those of us who were Jewish. Apparently, there were people housed in the facility who did not have much affection for us, and the administration didn't want us to be hurt. But as far as I was concerned, it was all the more reason to go. My team agreed, and the administration finally consented.

During our time in the facility, I shared my testimony and some music in a concert while the team gave out roses. One man spat full in Heatherly's face as she was offering him a rose. He went on to receive it without a trace of remorse. Heatherly walked away without a word. Only Beate, one of the German believers on the team, saw the incident. She immediately went to Heatherly and began washing and kissing her face—ministering to her in the Spirit in a sweet and humble way.

Later on, Jurgen and Heatherly were visiting people in their rooms. They came upon a woman who lay dying in her bed. She had thrown up on herself and the stench permeated the area. Jurgen offered the woman a rose and her whole face lit up. He got on his knees and began talking to her about how much Jesus loved her and how beautiful she was to God. He was wooing her to the Lord, amid the vomit and smell of death. This is the beauty of humility expressed in the German people—a precious thing—clearly something the enemy of our souls seeks to corrupt.

Many Germans have approached team members on these trips to express deep sorrow and regret for what happened in the Holocaust. Then they ask for forgiveness. At first I was careful—mindful of the position the Jewish community holds in terms of forgiveness—not to respond with those words. I don't believe I am the person they most need to seek forgiveness from. Only God can truly receive their heartfelt sorrow over the legacy of their people and country and set them free.

Later I pondered the whole subject of them asking my forgiveness. Why do they feel a need when they know they did not personally harm me? Maybe they are aware of an unwillingness to forgive in the Jewish community and they sense our judgment over generations. Maybe they intuit us tightening up when we hear their language or accent.

The Jewish argument is "they did not directly harm me, or my family, so I am not the person to offer forgiveness because I am not the actual victim." But then why do we act like we have been wronged by them? In my parents' generation many would pull back and think twice about buying German products, or connecting with Germans when they encountered them along the way, or traveling about in Germany. Even in my generation I have met some who feel similarly as my parents did and are raising their children to not buy German products. Certainly, this sentiment is much less than it was in the previous generation—but it still exists.

What if the Germans are only responding to subliminal messages we are sending, but for which we refuse to take responsibility?

If we are still holding some kind of judgment toward them—and prejudice for what their people did—is it not then appropriate for them to ask forgiveness, and for us to forgive? The Jewish people were already a minority before they were greatly diminished by the purposeful intent of the Nazis, who the Germans allowed to take over. The reality is our people suffered tremendous loss and Germany as a nation was made to recognize this. But there are also many individual Germans who have personally felt the deep need to acknowledge their genuine sorrow for the sins of their forbears and countrymen.

The truth is that the Holocaust is one of the single most powerful historical events that we as Jews identify with, and the Germans know we hold them accountable, even to this day. They are relentlessly schooled about what happened in the Holocaust, almost as if they should take the guilt of their fathers and grandfathers upon their own shoulders and their children's—as if it is an indelible legacy that cannot be erased or redeemed. Tattooed into the German soul forever. In effect, we continue to judge them for what was done and stand at a distance from them as a country and a culture. And that is part of why they ask our forgiveness. Should we not, then, be able to express forgiveness to them?

I know my family and I judged the Germans—not just the Nazis or that generation—and held them accountable, wanting nothing to do with them. But those of us who are Jewish by birth and believers in Jesus realize He paid for all the sins of mankind—even the great evils in this world. When any individual receives Him as Lord of their lives, they receive the unconditional forgiveness of God bought by Jesus' sacrifice on the cross. It is that same forgiveness all believers are encouraged to extend to others, that in the process we may also be healed.

Maybe we don't forgive because we can't believe any human being could do such terrible things. I think the Germans also find it overwhelming to believe their fathers, mothers, uncles, aunts, and grandparents are the ones who enacted these horrific events. That Germany, a deeply Christian nation, committed such heinous acts against family and friends, neighbors, bosses, employees. Against the men, women, and children who fought and struggled alongside them.

We, the Jewish people, have trouble envisioning ourselves as capable of such things.

But we are.

Everyone is in God's sight.

Scripture says so:

"For everyone has sinned; we all fall short of God's glorious standard."

(Romans 3:23—New Living Translation)

I believe we can all become instruments of evil under the right set of circumstances. Whether we act on our feelings or not is another story. It's amazing how we can find ways to justify what is evil when we feel it serves what is good. In other words, the ends justify the means.

It is in the acknowledgement of our common human sinfulness, our penchant to think and do evil, that we can look at our brothers, the Germans, and have mercy—even forgive. Our realization that we, too, are capable of being so deeply deceived and committing such incredible evil in the sight of God should sober and humble us, especially as we realize we are forgiven by our Creator, who loves us and wants to deliver us from our sin. I believe it is only in the wake of this pardon that we can begin to love one another.

Love is the single strongest weapon against anti-Semitism. Love touches the deep place of our humanity and reminds us that we are not automatons, but flesh and blood with soul and spirit, called to value and respect each other's existence, not destroy it.

But this perspective has become extremely relative. Our hearts are calloused. If we can destroy life in the womb because it's inconvenient and do away with those who are feeble and old, how can we expect to teach the next generation to cherish what we have trashed?

A few years ago I saw the Polish movie, *Aftermath*, loosely based on the book, *Neighbors*. The movie unfolds the story from a modern-day perspective. I waited through the credits to see if they would mention Jedwabne, but if they did I couldn't find it.

As I stood to leave I noticed one other woman in the theatre. She was much older and felt comfortable sharing her thoughts with me—a stranger. She thought it very brave for Polish people to make and release this movie. I said not all Polish people felt the same about this movie, as there had been a lot of controversy. She then revealed that she was a survivor—a Polish Jew. She was rescued with many of the Jewish children in Poland by some of the more courageous Polish people. I told her I had visited the real town this movie focused on, and there were all kinds of opinions about what actually happened.

She continued talking as we walked outside. I told her I was a Jewish believer in Jesus. Surprisingly she didn't seem offended. In fact, she was somewhat intrigued by Jesus because the Polish people who rescued her loved the Lord.

During our conversation she communicated how proud she was of the fact she taught her children not to hate. Yet as we dialogued further, she confessed that while on a cruise that stopped at a German village, she refused to get off the boat. She *couldn't*. She also declined monetary reparations from Germany. She said she *couldn't* look at a

German mark ever again. Finally, she shared how she had recently been invited to Berlin for a special survivor's conference, and admitted her uncertainty as to whether or not she would go.

I found her perspective frustrating because it seemed so conflicted. How could she say in one breath she taught her children not to hate and in the next tell me all the reasons she couldn't connect with anything or anyone German? Furthermore, she said the only reason she would ever visit Poland again was if she could find the people who rescued her all those years ago. I walked away from our exchange thinking this was a woman in denial who couldn't even see the contradictions in her own thinking.

I talked to Dusty, our oldest daughter, about what happened and she suggested something surprising. She gently presented the possibility that maybe the woman really *couldn't* look at anything German, because she had PTSD (Post Traumatic Stress Disorder). Of course! Why wouldn't she have PTSD? I still flinch when I hear or see larger dogs like German Shepherds or Doberman Pinchers. I shrink a little inside myself. It's been more than 50 years since I was bitten by the dog, but it's always with me.

How much more for survivors of something so horrific as the Holocaust? And yet it seems to create an impossible situation for Germans and Jews. Many survivors can't or won't have anything to do with Germans or Germany, and then the Germans are wounded by what they see as refusal and rejection.

Who can heal such a wound?

"Forgiveness has creative power to move us away from a past moment of pain, to unshackle us from our endless chain of reactions, and to create a new situation in which both the wrongdoer and the wronged can begin a new way... Forgiveness offers a chance at reconciliation; it is an opportunity for a life together instead of death together.

The alternative to reconciliation is, in the end, a ceaseless process of self-destruction. The brilliant American theologian, Reinhold Niebuhr, saw this after WWII and said: 'We must finally be reconciled with our foe, lest we both perish in the vicious circle of hatred.' There must be a release from the past or we are forever grounded on its unfair pain."

(Forgive and Forget: Healing the Hurts We Don't Deserve by Lewis B. Smedes*)*

15

HOW DO WE HEAL?

We are told in the Passover Haggadah—the book we read through for the Passover Seder—that we stand in the skin of our forefathers who passed through the Red Sea on dry land. If this is so, do we not also stand in the skin of those who were killed and almost killed in the Holocaust, even generations after? Is there not something in us that can speak love and forgiveness, one voice at a time to one person at a time? And in speaking that kind of grace to each one, are we not releasing them from the burden of generational judgment and condemnation?

Last time I checked, no one I know is greater than God. He alone is the Righteous Judge.

How do the Jewish people begin to heal? When do we look beyond the hurts of our past? Not forgetting, but perhaps needing to give those wounds to God so we can move on and experience healing in ourselves, in Germany, and possibly even the nations?

If, as believers, we continue to harbor offense we will certainly identify with our people as a race and nation, but fail in all we are meant to be as those called to be ambassadors of reconciliation and a light to the nations. Is it possible that in our failure to genuinely love and reconcile with those we once perceived as enemies, we may unknowingly help further the seed of anti-Semitism by sowing resentment and bitterness in the hearts of those sincerely seeking some kind of forgiveness, healing, and closure?

If we are not offended, then there really is no need to forgive. However, from what I have seen in people I know or have met—Jews and Gentiles who love Israel—there is a sense of irreparable wounding in regard to Germany and the Holocaust.

As believers we do not have the luxury of retaining that perspective, no matter how valid it may seem in our culture and heritage. The blood of a holy God was given for every offense and sin once and for all, so that none might perish, but all might come into everlasting life through Messiah Jesus. Harboring offense hinders the expression of God's love in and through us, His very invitation, to those people we continue to judge in our hearts.

When Ananias was called upon to pray for Saul of Tarsus, he was more than a little concerned. Saul was a monster pursuing brand new followers of The Way, persecuting, imprisoning, perhaps even murdering in his zeal. Was it any wonder Ananias had a few questions for the Lord? He had no earthly reason to go see Saul—but God. And in his complete obedience, Ananias witnessed a transformation. A heart of stone became a heart of flesh. The monster became a man.

Are we not called to do the same? To extend the same unconditional love and pardon we received? It was given before we had any understanding of our need for it. It was provided long before we knew enough to be sorry. This is the way of God. Our forgiveness isn't predicated on someone's apology or repentance. It is based on the absolution given long ago through the atoning work of Messiah. Our forgiveness toward others is an act of worship, a reverent echo of our King and Liberator, the Holy One of Israel. He forgave us all our sins and delivered us from the bondage of our only real enemy long before we knew enough to pray and ask.

My father, who I thought of as a monster because of his rage, became a man again when I saw him through the lens of God's love and mercy and showed compassion toward him. Ultimately, I believe it was because of that pardon and reconciliation that my dad came to faith in Jesus. But there is no guarantee with love or forgiveness. It must be offered freely and without fear or expectation, trusting in God and His love for us. It may or may not be received, but the scripture assures us in 1 Corinthians 13 that "Love never fails."

"But I say to you who hear: Love your enemies, do good to those who hate you, bless those who curse you, and pray for those who spitefully use you. To him who strikes you on the one cheek, offer the other also. And from him who takes away your cloak, do not withhold your tunic either. Give to everyone who asks of you. And from him who takes away your goods do not ask them back. And just as you want men to do to you, you also do to them likewise. But if you love those who love you, what credit is that to you? For even sinners love those who love them. And if you do good to those who do good to you, what credit is that to you? For even sinners do the same. And if you lend to those from whom you hope to receive back, what credit is that to you? For even sinners lend to sinners to receive as much back. But love your enemies, do good and lend, hoping for nothing in return; and your reward will be great, and you will be sons of the Most High. For He is kind to the unthankful and evil. Therefore be merciful, just as your Father also is merciful."

(Luke 6:27-36)

16

A NEW DIRECTION?

Somewhere in the middle of 2014, while worshiping at my friend's church in Lynwood, California, the Lord spoke a single word into my spirit: *Palestine.*

I had just returned from a profound experience with *A Tour of Roses* in Munich and Mauthausen and was still recovering, even as we began planning for our Poland project in the fall. As I poured out my heart in worship and prayer, I was sure I must have heard incorrectly. Scripturally it didn't make any sense. Culturally it was offensive and politically unthinkable. I remember responding, "Surely You must mean Israel?"

Silence.

As the word hung in the air I began to realize that in this case it represented how the people living there identify themselves and their location. Whether or not it was scripturally, politically, or culturally correct wasn't relevant in this situation. What mattered was God revealing to me how they identify themselves.

A few weeks later I felt the Lord impress on me this thought: *These are my people also and I have not forgotten them.* The moment the idea crystallized in my psyche I absolutely knew it did not originate with me, which could only mean one thing. God was calling me to go. As I considered the slowly accumulating evidence of His invitation, the sheer insanity of doing a project in Israel, let alone trying to reach out to Palestinians, loomed huge and impossible. I decided it might be a good idea to talk with our associate pastor, Lynn Cory.

Lynn has led three ministry trips to Israel beginning in 2004. I reluctantly participated in each when it became obvious God was the One beckoning. Each tour exposed layers of revelation, links in the chain of God's work in my life.

Years before, my dad had offered Michael and me free round-trip tickets to see "The Land." Like almost all Jewish parents, Dad deeply desired I set foot in Eretz (the land of) Israel. But I had zero desire. And it hadn't increased a whit by the time Lynn had asked me to lead worship on that first trip. But God intervened and made it clear He was doing the inviting.

I still remember everyone on the bus singing "songs of ascent" as we approached Jerusalem. My heart was hard and cynical. If God could meet us anywhere at all, why should Jerusalem be such a big deal? The Temple no longer existed and now we knew the Lord as Emmanuel—God with us!

I continued with something of an oppositional point of view until my roommate and I settled into our accommodations and I stepped out on the balcony facing Bethlehem. Abruptly I was in the presence of the Lord, as if I had suddenly stepped from the street into the Holy of Holies, and was facedown before my King. There was no denying He was in this place. Whether it made any sense to me or not, the Lord made it clear that Jerusalem was a special place of His habitation.

I wrestled with a great many things during the trip, and at the end I was sitting by the Mediterranean on a cold January morning before traveling to the airport. I said to the Lord in my heart, *OK. I went. I saw. I'm done.*

He responded, *I love you, My daughter, and you'll be back.*

And so it was. I returned twice more under Lynn's leadership.

Now, as I wrestled with what I felt the Lord was leading me toward, Lynn seemed the best person to ask for prayer.

I shared how it seemed God was moving me to bring roses to the Palestinians. He began praying, asking God to help me hear Him. And I did, even as Lynn continued petitioning, but the words that surfaced in my soul were not easy.

... and they loved not their lives...

(Revelation 12:11)

This is from a passage about martyrdom. That was how I first understood it, but then perceived the Lord smoothing it out, helping me comprehend what He was speaking to me through the verse at this time. The New Living Translation says it best:

"And they did not love their lives so much that they were afraid to die."

At first all I could think about was how much I still loved my life on Planet Earth, was rather attached to it, and not really ready to sacrifice it—even for God. But literal martyrdom was not the actual issue. Up until that moment all the projects for *A Tour of Roses* were predicated on events that took place in the past, whether the Holocaust or—as in the case of our project in Belfast—The Troubles. In this situation the problem at hand was the present-day, overt, ongoing violence and conflict between the Palestinians and Israelis. And for me, that generated a far more primal fear.

17

SPYING OUT THE LAND

"So do not fear, for I am with you; do not be dismayed, for I am your God. I will strengthen you and help you; I will uphold you with my righteous right hand."

(Isaiah 41:10)

From the moment the Lord began speaking about this particular *A Tour of Roses* project until the morning we boarded our planes for Tel Aviv the processing, planning, and prayer that went into this spanned almost two years. It was the single most challenging project I have ever done.

I am not an administrative-type person, and there was a ton of odds and ends to attend to. At one point, the Lord spoke to my heart about the gift of tenacity. Not exactly listed among those spiritual gifts mentioned in the book of Corinthians, but a serious necessity when God beckons you to a mission somewhere no human has invited you to go.

I cannot tell you how many people, in subtle and not-so-subtle ways, suggested I might be mistaken about timing, location, or perhaps about going at all. But, convinced God was calling, I realized the essential issue was obedience, despite how impossible it seemed at the time.

In early January 2015 my good friend, Evi, accompanied me again, this time to Jerusalem to spend a week or so praying and "scouting out the land." We holed up in an eclectic little hostel in the Old City, right in the middle of the Shuk (marketplace)—and within walking distance of an Aroma cafe—Yum!

It was snowing in Jerusalem and very cold. One thing which always surfaces in my mind each time I reflect on our visit is walking through the Shuk in the Christian Arab section. All the vendors were very welcoming with hot tea of my choice, sitting me down and talking their spiel. There was a deep thread of hospitality, even as they welcomed me to play their game of negotiation. In stark contrast, the Israeli peddlers were often abrupt with very little time for welcome or play. They were much more focused on getting to the point of sale. While the Israeli sellers were reputed to be more honest and straight-forward about their wares, the Arabs welcomed each potential customer with the same hospitality—sometimes even a little nosh—before they started talking their trade. The genuine kindness and warmth of the Arab vendors really struck a chord with me.

Our plan was to pray in Jerusalem and hopefully find a way to visit Bethlehem, although I didn't have a clue how that would happen. But one of the first things I did when we actually settled into our digs in the Old City was visit the Western Wall, aka the Wailing Wall. It is the remnant of the outside enclosure of the temple area. People gather from all over the world to pray, touching the stones and cramming their little folded paper petitions and wishes into the gaps of that ancient partition as if the stones themselves have power to grant the desires of their hearts.

Don't get me wrong, I always feel His presence in this place. I am not even sure why. And I, too, feel a deep longing to connect in prayer as I touch the stones. But He is not *in* the stones. Not even in the cracks and crevices. And yet, somehow, His Presence is there in a special way.

I took a chair and sat back a distance, waiting. And when I heard, the words were quiet and firm, spoken deep into my soul. And I knew they were non-negotiable.

I will not hold you guiltless if you do not move and speak in what I have called you to.

This was not what I expected to hear. Promises, assurances, reminders of His love for me, and His faithfulness. That's what I anticipated. Who He is and who He is calling me to be, these were the assurances my heart desired, not a warning. Yet this was clearly God's word to me. It continued to sound loud and long after I backed out from the Wall and walked away.

We connected with an associate pastor from Living Bread International Church in East Jerusalem. The pastor talked about their work in the Palestinian refugee camp, Dheisheh, and I was immediately drawn to the idea of reaching out to them. Evi and I worshiped with them, and the pastor said she would let me know when they were going into Bethlehem next.

As it turned out, Evi had to fly home sooner than I did. She left on Friday. I drove her to the airport thinking I had most likely missed my only opportunity to get into Bethlehem and the refugee camp before Monday. But God had other plans.

I stayed in Tel Aviv at the newly opened Moishe Rosen Center. This was Jews for Jesus' hospitality/evangelism center that was named for their founder. A call came after Evi left. Saturday would work out for me to visit Bethlehem if I could get into East Jerusalem by a certain time. Gratefully, I accepted the invitation without a second thought and made plans to leave Tel Aviv fairly early so I could arrive without any stress.

Everything—and I do mean everything—conspired to keep me from reaching my destination the next morning. Roads were blocked off because of snow in Jerusalem. Traffic moved very slowly in some places. Thankfully, I was able to text the pastor about my situation. She was very kind and reassured me, saying that whenever I arrived I should park the car somewhere in Jersualem and head to the bus station in East Jerusalem. Later that morning, one of the roads became accessible and I was allowed to drive through.

As I parked the car and walked over to the bus station, I texted the pastor, saying I was on my way. Stories of bombs and busses flitted through my head. I felt tension rising as I searched for the correct bus. The Arab driver was kind. Because it was the Sabbath I walked through the checkpoint in Bethlehem without any problems. The pastor and her friend waved to me as I emerged on the other side.

Pastor Karen's friend, Arif, was very considerate. He and Karen escorted me around Bethlehem as I explained a little about *A Tour of Roses*, some of our past projects, and what I hoped might happen in Bethlehem. Arif was a brand-new believer and though he was drawn to the whole idea of kindness, he was also scared. The pastor kept encouraging him and me, reiterating that it would all work out just fine. But Arif was not convinced. The fear I perceived in him also concerned me. Arif was particularly tense about the idea of me identifying myself as a Jew while giving out the roses. He asked me not to share that information with anyone while he was in our company.

Arif had a home in Dheisheh. The refugee camp was like a small city with about 15,000 people surviving on different levels of financial provision. Trash and graffiti cluttered the streets, and buildings everywhere had been defaced. The darkness and oppression were palpable.

Arif welcomed us into his house where I met his daughter and son. His daughter was especially kind. They cooked a meal for us on an open fire inside the house and made special dishes from scratch because the daughter was studying to be a chef.

Sometime later, Arif offered to take me into the main area of Dheisheh where most of the shops were located. He needed a haircut. I saw many men wearing Arafat kerchiefs and it frightened me. Their faces appeared so hard and unforgiving. Fear was a factor as I walked those streets. Arif was afraid because I was Jewish and I was afraid because he was afraid. I didn't see Jesus that day as we walked. I saw what I feared.

When we returned, dinner was ready and we continued talking. It all felt so oppressive, even though Arif and his daughter were very hospitable and kind. Several times he asked the pastor and me to stay the night as his guests, but I became very uncomfortable with that idea. I needed to leave.

It seemed an eternity until Arif's brother came by with his wife and offered to drive us back into Jerusalem. By then I was physically nauseous and convinced there was no way on earth I could possibly bring *ATOR* to Dheisheh. I was so grateful when we set foot in Jerusalem, and even more so when I returned to Tel Aviv safely and fell into bed. I was exhausted in every conceivable way and felt sick inside.

Early Sunday morning I dressed and began walking through the streets of Tel Aviv, especially out by the beach, processing everything I had seen and heard with the Lord—especially Dheisheh. I thought about the men with the kerchiefs and Arif's fear. The Lord impressed on me how stark the white stone buildings were and how stunning red roses would appear in the quantities we would bring. It was deep into the afternoon before I was fully able to connect again to God's love and respond to His calling in obedience and trust. At that point His direction and timing became very clear.

"To the pure, all things are pure, but to those who are corrupted and do not believe, nothing is pure." (Titus 1:15). For me, this speaks especially of how we look at people. Are we looking for Jesus at work in or around them? Are we listening to what the Holy Spirit is telling us as we engage? Or are we stumbled by what we might see in their faces or hear in their words or voices.

Every human being belongs to God, even if they have signed on directly with the enemy for a season. Every human being was created by God out of His love for us. The Lord wants to use our hearts, hands, and feet to reach out with His love, even to those we might think the least likely. But that can only happen as we look with His eyes and His love.

The next day I flew home, the Lord's words at the Wall still reverberating in my soul.

During the fourth watch of the night, Jesus went out to them, walking on the sea. When the disciples saw Him walking on the sea, they were terrified. "It's a ghost!" they said, and cried out in fear.

But Jesus immediately spoke up: "Take courage! It is I. Do not be afraid."

"Lord, if it is You," Peter replied, "command me to come to You on the water."

"Come," said Jesus.

Then Peter got down out of the boat, walked on the water, and came toward Jesus.

(Matthew 14:25-29—The Berean Study Bible)

18

WALKING ON WATER

When I think about it in retrospect, the entire project was completely crazy. I have always struggled with the concept of being a team player, let alone a captain. It's so much easier traveling alone, or with Michael and the girls, than with a group of people made up of friends and other strangers.

Soon after I made applications for the Israel project available, I realized this would be the largest group I had ever led. When all was said and done there were sixteen people who were directly part of my team, along with three individuals from Holy Land Missions. Holy Land Missions was the only Palestinian Christian ministry that had agreed to help us in a supportive role, particularly as we reached out in Bethlehem and the refugee camp. I knew God would shepherd us through the process, I just didn't know what it would look like. Several in our group had never participated in an *ATOR* project before. It seemed like almost every person hailed from a different cultural background: Jewish, Palestinian, Puerto Rican, German, Polish—even Native American. Thankfully my dear friends, Jurgen and Elaine, each stepped up as team pastors. I was very grateful.

I originally met Khalida, a Palestinian believer, probably a month or so prior to making a final decision about who would be on the team. Mutual friends had suggested we connect so we went to lunch together. During the afternoon it became clear very quickly that Khalida was a major extrovert. The more outgoing she proved to be, the more withdrawn I became. And yet, it was obvious she had a tremendous heart for Jewish evangelism. It surprised her when I informed her that the heart of this particular *ATOR* project was actually focused on her people—the Palestinians.

My lunch with Khalida gave me pause for thought. I wondered how this would work out with all the different personalities involved. But God was speaking to me about loving people more than roses, and caring for them more than my concern as to how we were going to work with 7,500 red roses. And He wasn't talking about the Palestinians or Israelis we would encounter. He was talking about my team. He emphasized that either we did this project all together or we didn't do it at all. In other words, unity was key. That was a particularly hard word for me to accept since I had been so accustomed to doing things on my own. But it was the key to our survival and success on this project.

The roses were an entirely other situation. On all previous trips I had no problem purchasing them in large quantities from the growers or wholesale florists in the area. But as I contacted some of the Israeli growers, I discovered roses were in scarce supply. I began to consider importing roses from somewhere else, but my good friend, Jurgen, encouraged me to bless Israel by buying from them.

Michael and I were praying one evening and I was in tears—so worried about how we would locate enough roses for the project. The Lord gave him a picture of me on a fishing boat on the Sea of Galilee. There was a heavy fog and I was standing out on deck trying to see through it, obviously searching for something. The fog slowly began to lift and then Michael saw the Sea was filled with red roses. I cried. Almost all the growers I talked to who knew anything about roses said it would be impossible to find that many roses at one time. But I knew the Lord was reassuring me that He had this detail covered and I would not lack in this department. And so it was.

I decided to try something different and call some of the retail florists in Jerusalem. The first shop I contacted was Dalia Flowers, the oldest flower shop in all Israel—established in 1934. I couldn't believe they were willing to compete with the growers' prices. One of the owners was quite taken with what we were doing. He visited the website for *ATOR*, read about the project, and listened to some of our music. He personally delivered the first batch of roses to us in Jerusalem. We became friends. We purchased 5,000 of our roses from Dalia Flowers and another 2,500 from a grower I connected with soon after. In total, we gave out 7,500 roses during our project in Israel in 2016.

People ask me, from time to time, about the timing of these projects. I don't decide that on my own. It is a matter of prayer. And while I was winding up my time in Tel Aviv on my little scouting trip in January 2015, the Lord showed me this project would take place during Purim 2016. But it wasn't until we were pretty deep into the preparations that I realized the week of Purim included Easter that year. Concern blossomed in regard to how crazy tensions might get between Israelis and Palestinians during our stay in Jerusalem. The idea of bodyguards surfaced as a viable consideration, and then we had to let it go. We were in the Lord's hands—as always.

3/17/2016

The first day we went out very briefly on the streets of the Old City in Jerusalem, giving out roses with Arabic cards on them. 200-300 roses were gone in about 20 minutes, or the length of three songs.

There were many smiles and questions. What I loved best was when a young Jewish man brought over his friends to look at the back of one of the team member's t-shirts and comment positively. I had specially designed the back with a picture of a long stem rose down the middle, and in Hebrew and Arabic on either side of the rose were the words of the Aaronic Benediction from Numbers 6:24-26. I heard some people cried and were very touched.

Sheilah shared how a vacationing Nordic couple came up to her for a rose. Sheilah said, "They were believers and were so touched by what we were doing, they began crying."

Magda related how she gave a rose to two Greek orthodox women all dressed in black robes and told them, "This is for you because God loves you." They took the roses from her and gave her a very touching hug.

Karen shared how she was giving out roses with Jurgen when a shopkeeper asked them why they were doing this. Jurgen said it was to show love to both Jews and Arabs. The shopkeeper gave Jurgen a big hug and said, "Thank you. This war is so hard for all of us. No one wins at wartime."

3/18/2016

Not only was it Easter week during Purim, but there was also a marathon passing through Jerusalem. There were 25,000 people running, 1,800 security officers, and it was themed, *"Tikkun Olam"* (Healing the World). On top of that, it turned out we arrived in Bethlehem just in time to celebrate Arabic Mother's Day. God's timing is always amazing!

As Sam began handing out roses, one of the police called him and his teammate over. The officer said, "Why are you here? What group are you with? Who told you to do this?"

Sam answered, "We are here to say God loves you, and we are here to say we love the people of Israel."

The policeman said, "Let me see the card." When he read the card he got a big smile on his face and said, "Thank you very much, Sir." He shook Sam's hand, then radioed the rest of the police that our group was ok.

Gayle saw one of the marathon runners cut clear over to the gated fence. He was just standing there waiting for a rose. Finally, someone gave him a rose and he took off and continued running. The Lord spoke to Gayle's heart, *See there, the runners want the roses too.* So, he went and stood at the fence and stretched his arm out with a rose, and the runners started taking roses from him. It wasn't long till he was out of roses. There were two or three other team members nearby with armloads of roses, watching the runners go by. He told them to hold out a rose. They began doing that and were out of roses in no time.

A woman took a rose from Elaine and smiled at her companion. They asked Elaine, "What is this for?"

She answered, "This is an expression of the love of God to you today."

Elaine offered it to her companion also, but he explained they would share the rose. The woman then said, "You do not know what this means to us... We just lost someone very dear to us."

Elaine asked whom they had lost, and the woman shared that it was a family member. Elaine then offered to pray for them, which surprised them, but they said ok. Afterward, as the woman got up to leave, the man, who had been mostly quiet, got up and opened his arms to Elaine and hugged her. The woman said, "You just don't know how much this means to us; you will never know."

3/19/2016

Mazzen shared that as soon as he went out the door of the hotel he gave a rose to a woman and her Israeli boyfriend. The woman asked in Spanish, "Do you speak Spanish? Why are you doing this?"

Mazzen responded, "It is because we want to express the love of God to the people." The woman was from Mexico and Catholic. Mazzen began explaining to her how Jesus died on the cross and shed his blood for her so that she would not perish. She gave him a big hug. Then Mazzen talked to her boyfriend who was Israeli. He said, "I am a Palestinian from Ramallah and I just want to say that I love you." The boyfriend gave Mazzen a hug and shook his hand. It was apparent how moved he was.

3/20/2016

Palm Sunday morning we hung out with the Palestinian church in Jerusalem, pastored by Steven Khoury of Holy Land Missions. Khalida was kind enough to translate for me between songs and I shared some of my testimony with the people. From there we returned to our hotel and gathered our luggage to cross over into Bethlehem to stay at the lovely Holy Land Hotel. The management was extremely generous, giving us a wonderful room for the roses where we could work on them at no extra charge. Early in the planning for this project I had reasoned we should stay in Jerusalem the whole time because I thought it would be safer. But my friend, Mary, really spoke to the fear behind that, and I know now it was God correcting my course. He made it clear that it was not enough to go and minister in Bethlehem by day and stay in Jerusalem at night. I knew it was the smallness of my heart and fear that kept me from seeing how big our God is and how much He wanted to pour out in and through us.

3/21/2016

One of the special events we agreed to participate in was an Arabic Mother's Day brunch at a very upscale hotel in Bethlehem. There were many women at the brunch. At first I felt rather unsure about what I was supposed to do and who was supposed to speak— Khalida or me. It seemed they wanted only my songs and preferred Khalida to speak to them. But as the main message was given, the Lord spoke to my heart and I realized I needed to step forward. They were not asking, but I needed to step forward anyway. This was the moment, especially since there was no other concert scheduled. The main speaker was the pastor's wife. She was speaking of family and the mother's place.

As she continued I realized that I had a place to stand as a mom, one who has dealt with conflict and misunderstanding because of the issues of autism with our girls. The Lord also put on my heart to go up with Khalida as a sister, holding her hand as a symbol and picture of what I wanted to say. So I took her hand in mine and we shared the microphone as she translated for me.

"Good Morning," Khalida greeted the women in Arabic.

"Good Morning," I followed suit in Hebrew.

I proceeded to identify us as Jew and Palestinian, Bethlehem being Khalida's place of birth. As I tentatively continued, I shared some of my thoughts: "Some of you may have reacted when I said I was Jewish, but I believe God has made us one in Messiah."

Later I also shared about being a mom with three daughters who all struggle with some form of autism. One woman immediately connected. She stood up to speak.

"I have an adult child who has autism and sometimes I wish he were dead."

I related some of my struggle with our girls and another woman asked, "How do you handle that?"

I responded, "I can only handle it by abiding in the love of God. My children have changed me, softened my heart, brought me a compassion that I didn't have and didn't even want. They are teaching me to see differently."

I spoke about how our daughters all had similar problems but expressed them very differently. I shared, "In my opinion this is also true of us as Jews and Arabs. There are similar wounds of rejection in both peoples but we react, process, and express them very differently. When we become believers, God wants us to see each other with His heart."

After lunch the team divided into two groups. One group hit the streets of Bethlehem. The second group went with the scouts from the Bethlehem church to the hospitals in Beit Jala.

Heatherly related that the hospitals were "sooooooooo open." She encountered one man sitting on a bench in the hallway. He was dressed in traditional Palestinian clothing and headscarf. Daniel who was helping us with all the protocol as we interacted with the Palestinians, was unsure if he would receive a rose from a woman, so he handed the rose to the man and then walked down the hall.

Heatherly sat with the bucket of roses and replenished the team as needed. She was sitting ten feet from the man as he read and reread his card. Finally, he stood up and approached her, and motioned for a second rose and she gave it to him. He then took the two roses into the room and gave them to his family. He came back for one more rose for himself and returned to his bench. He sat there staring at the card for a long time.

The team met up with a Catholic group from Croatia. We connected with their priest, who loved Jesus. He asked Jurgen if the team and I could give their group roses. We all met in the chapel and the priest asked me to sing a song and share my testimony. We were sharing in three languages: Croatian to German, German to English, and then English to German, and German to Croatian. We were all touched and Jesus knit us together in love. After my testimony, there was a time of questions. One of the questions from their group was "How can *our* wounds get healed?" Several people from the team shared their experiences with healing. Jurgen shared how beautiful it was to see how God united Catholic believers with us and made us one in His spirit.

Sheilah reflected on how there is such a hunger for the gift of love in this place. She noticed how the team barely made it out the front doors of the hotel and all the roses were handed out. "We literally stopped traffic on both sides of the road. Cars were lined up in both directions as we ran to hand each person a rose. Many smiles and thanks were a blessing to our hearts."

Just prior to handing out our roses on the street, a Muslim man prayed to receive Jesus and joined us in handing out roses. He had the biggest smile on his face!

3/22/2016

At the refugee camp, Dheisheh, the first responders were children. The roses were kind of amazing to them at first. But then a certain level of greediness and desperation took over and there was no sharing among them. At the same time there seemed to be a genuine curiosity about the singing. Pastor Steve kept shooing them away after they got roses, but they kept coming back. So, we eventually moved to the main street. He had me set up my keyboard and stand in a memorial spot where several Palestinians were shot and killed. As I was singing, about 25-30 kids and some young adults gathered. I remembered a word given to me before we left, that what we were doing was not about this generation so much as it was about the children.

As I sang, I looked into their faces and they were like little flowers, soaking up sun, soaking up love, in a very dry and thirsty place. I realized I had an opportunity to say something to them, especially since Pastor Steve was not afraid to translate for me.

"I am Jewish," I told them. "My heart was once very hard, but God touched my heart and changed it, and filled me with His love. My friends and I are here to share this same love with you, through the roses and the songs, because we believe God loves you and He loves us too. And although it is very hard between us Jews and Palestinians right now, God wants us to learn how to love each other."

One young woman wearing a head covering in the back of the crowd shouted back, "I love you, too!" And then all the kids clapped.

Randy saw a carpenter working on his building in Dheisheh as we walked up the street. Randy handed him a rose. On the way back when he walked by the same building, Randy waved to the carpenter who looked at him, and threw him a kiss, saying: "Habibi." Randy shared, "It's the only Arabic word I know. It means love."

In the evening we decided to prayer-walk Manger Square. This turned out to be exactly what was needed. As I sang in an archway, the team walked the square and prayed. Three women heard a voice singing and it called to them. They felt compelled to come closer. Brenda, Elaine, and Khalida were able to speak with them and as the Muslim call to prayer sounded overhead, the women prayed to the living God for salvation.

Sam and Heatherly stood with Khalida as she spoke with about five men. Heatherly shared: "They were accusing Christians of idolatry.

Khalida proceeded to explain the trinity. A Palestinian daughter of the Most High living God quoted the Shema (Taken from Deuteronomy 6:4, 'Hear, O Israel: The Lord our God, the Lord is one.') in Hebrew to Muslim men while standing in front of the Church of the Nativity. Only God could orchestrate this."

On the ride back, Jurgen, Khalida, Sam and Heatherly rode in a taxi. Heatherly told us later: "The driver had a similar orphan story as Khalida's and his heart was open and the spirit was sweet and gentle. Jurgen went to get the driver a rose. Khalida was privileged to pray with him. Sam and I just sat there and cried."

3/23/2016

Before we left the hotel, Mazzen had an encounter: "I went out on the balcony, and a Palestinian man from America came out with his mother. We greeted each other and began talking. I explained why we were here, and about the countries our group was from. We weren't here to convert anyone, but to bring hope. He opened up and said he was here because there was some land the family sold. He was there to take them to court and had issues in the family. He was questioning Islam because he sees no love in Islam, and he had questions about the Bible. He asked why are there so many books in the Old and New Testaments in the Bible. I explained the Bible and the Word of God, and how Jeremiah was a book, and each book has a name. How Paul used to persecute Christians and God encountered Paul on the way to Damascus. At the end I asked him what he thought about this. He said it was very beautiful. We parted."

We traveled in groups by taxi to Manger Square the next day. I quickly set up my keyboard and started worshiping as the team began handing out roses. A young woman from one of the shops was listening to every song. When I took a break, she came out and gave Sam her rose back and said, "Here—for peace."

I felt like I should follow up with her. So when the roses were all gone. I went into her shop and said, "So I guess you figured out what we are doing."

She responded, "I knew what you were doing from the beginning." Her face seemed rather hard.

I continued, "Well, I am Jewish and I believe in Jesus and I came here to share that love with you."

She replied, "You want to share that love with me? Why don't you take down the walls and stop killing my family?"

I responded, "I have no power to do that but we do the things we can do, which is to come here and share His love."

I talked about how I have visited men in prison, who had life sentences. Some were bound by the physical cage, and some of them were free, even though they were still physically confined. She said, "Why not take the roses to them (the Israelis), they need it."

I said, "We did, but now we are bringing them to you. You can have all these external events going on and have peace. He can take the hurt from your heart. That is what the wounds are for, for Jesus to heal you."

Her face during our conversation became much softer and different. Then Sam, who was with me, said to her, "I want to say something, too. Please forgive us for the hurt that we caused your people." He was crying.

And she said, "You don't have to apologize."

He said, "No, I am really sorry." We could see it surprised and touched her, and her face softened even more.

By the time Khalida arrived, the team had already given out three buckets of roses. She started talking with two guys, and it grew to four, six, and then ten. She wound up talking with the main group about hatred, and about wanting peace. Khalida shared that one man was really listening, "I asked if he wanted this kind of life for his future children. He said he did not want his children to be full of hatred and mad at the Jewish people. So I shared with them about the Lord and Jesus removing hatred. They said, 'Oh we get it. We know what you are saying and want God to remove our hatred."' Khalida prayed with all six to receive the Lord.

Near the end of the day, Khalida was talking with two young boys. One was an orphan and told his story. Khalida responded by sharing her history as an orphan, and that she was from Bethlehem. Both boys prayed with her to receive the Lord.

Heatherly gave a rose to a small six-year-old girl and later told us the rest of the story: "She got halfway around the block and came back. She first said in Arabic, 'Two?' I held up one finger, only one rose. So, she tried in English a tiny 'Two' sound. Again I said one. She gave me big eyes and a pouty lip, 'Two?' I caved, but only so far. I took all the half-sized broken stemmed roses off the top of Sally's keyboard—about 4-5 pretty roses, but not ones we could pass out—and gave her all of those. Her response was so unexpected—these big huge eyes and a look of surprise. All she wanted was two and now she had so many. Her sweet spirit and gratitude melted my heart. I wanted to give her *everything!*"

Mallory was passing roses out on the far side of the square with Brenda. Brenda offered a rose to a man but he refused. Later the same man came back and said, "Ma'am, please forgive me. I was wrong to reject the rose." Mallory and Brenda were then able to share about the rose and how it represented God's love. He said he was a Muslim and shared about his wife being a Christian. He was there visiting his family.

They said, "Well one of your wife's prayers is being answered today, because this is a divine appointment and it isn't a mistake that we are both here in the square today."

3/24/2016

Daniel was kind enough to ferry us back out through the checkpoint by Bethlehem in three trips. The Palestinian Authority and the IDF (Israeli Defense Force) run the checkpoint and it can be difficult at times to go in and especially to go back out on the Israeli side. Once we were outside the checkpoint on the Israeli side, we called one of our Palestinian cabbie friends to come and get us all. Back in the Old City, we stashed our luggage at the Christ Church Guesthouse and immediately set out for the Garden Tomb, the generally accepted Protestant site of Jesus' burial and resurrection. Having visited the Garden Tomb each time I have been in Jerusalem, I find it amazing there can be such a place in the midst of such conflict and violence as there often is in East Jerusalem. I am always thankful for the peace I feel in that garden. It reaches a deep part of me and I hoped the team would also experience the garden in a similar way as we took time to reflect, worship, and take communion together.

From the Garden Tomb we walked through a little bit of East Jerusalem, and across the street to Damascus Gate. This has been a location where several people have been attacked, and the IDF stopped all vendors from selling outside the gate where we were. In fact, it looked pretty barren in some ways. All the color was gone with the vendors and their wares. But I felt the Lord lay on my heart a time of worship and prayer for us as a team there.

I was amazed no one stopped me as I took out my keyboard on the steps, turned it on, and began worshiping with a team member named Nic playing mandolin. It was, for me, an incredibly meaningful moment because we were sitting in a place of violence and loss. Yet as we worshiped God we could all feel His presence and peace.

That night was Purim, which was more like Halloween than anything else. I had heard that people dress in costumes, not just from the book of Esther, and that the holiday was an opportunity for partying and mischief. A young woman at the desk where we were staying, Christ Church Guesthouse, also joined us as we set out to share the roses. She led us out to Ben Yehuda Street, about a 20-minute walk.

Thirteen of us gave out roses along both sides of the street. A lot of people were open, even the Jewish people who seemed more religious and less celebratory. But on the way back we picked up a lot of cards broken off the roses and saw stems and heads of roses on the street. Maybe 30-40 cards and 20 roses, but we probably gave away 500 roses that night. For all the cards we picked up that were rejected, I prayed for the people who read them and tore them off. One person read the card and threw it in Khalida's face. It was not easy to love some of the people.

One man I gave a rose to asked why we were giving them out. I said, "Because God loves you."

And he said, "What God?"

I said, "The Maker of the Heavens and the Earth."

He said he didn't believe in God. He believed in humanity and the ability of people to heal themselves. I responded it was a limited ability. He explained it is religion that causes all the trouble. And I responded it is not God who is causing the problem but how people interpret Him. I shared with him that I know Him to be Love.

He informed me, "I am Jewish."

I said, "Me too. But I believe Jesus, Yeshua, is the Messiah—the Promised One."

Then he challenged me, "So only people who believe in Him are going to be OK."

I said, "You can choose."

He had been very hurt by religious people who were condescending to him, but he was quick to say he didn't feel that from me. But he didn't believe in God either.

We talked awhile and the team was praying for us as we dialogued, but his heart was very wounded. He had been in Hebron when two more people were stabbed and he said this is a crazy country—because of religion. And I said, "But that's not the same as God. And maybe one day you can ask God to show Himself to you. I did and He changed my heart. Not church—but God."

He offered me the rose back and I looked at him and said you can keep it. And he held onto it.

As we all walked back we ran into a group of young women who stopped us. Their leader, Sarah, asked what we were all about and I explained we were giving out roses as a way of sharing God's love. She was good with that until I told her we had also given roses to the Palestinians in Bethlehem. Then she was angry. She spoke about how she wanted the terrorists to all die. And I told her about the children that gathered around me in the refugee camp as I sang on the corner to them and we gave out roses—and then I told them I was Jewish and how God wants us to love one another. She really listened to us and we really listened to her. In the end, Sarah and I hugged each other.

Afterward, Mazzen and Khalida each identified themselves as Palestinians who love her and her people. She seemed a little surprised by that. Khalida went so far as to apologize for the hurt Sarah had suffered at the hands of her people. Again, I think Sarah was surprised. She and Khalida also hugged each other.

Heatherly and Yara began giving roses straight out of the hotel. They gave one to a man who stopped them, asking what organization they were with. They explained they were part of an international group sharing the love of God through roses.

He said, "What God?"

They said, "The God of Israel and Yeshua the Messiah."

He would not make eye contact throughout. Then he began shouting at the top of his lungs while pointing at them, "These people are missionaries. They are going against Israeli law."

Heatherly and Yara blessed him and kept walking.

Then one of the Arab vendors who knew our group walked up to his face and said, "Why are you shouting? These people are giving us beautiful roses and spreading peace. We need this in Israel. Stop shouting like that."

While handing out roses, Heatherly and another team member approached a Palestinian man sitting at an outdoor cafe in Jerusalem. He refused the rose but said, "I have a question for you. How many roses are you distributing? My question is why do you not bring bread and food to help the people? Why not bring something they really need?"

They responded, "Yes, we understand, but you see the faces of the people? They also need hope and joy, and we are trying to bring some of that."

He was still very contemplative but he took a rose.

They had some amazing responses that night, but there were also people who were very angry. One man took his rose apart petal by petal to get a response. Heatherly told him, "You act as if you are tearing apart MY rose. But that rose is yours. It was given to you. You are only tearing apart your own gift."

Heatherly told one girl *"Ani ohevet Yisrael"* (I love Israel) and that she didn't speak much more Hebrew than that.

The girl responded, "I think that is the most beautiful thing you can learn to say in Hebrew."

3/25/2016

We divided up into groups of 4-5 and went to several points around Jerusalem. Heatherly's team went to Jaffa gate. They had a really sweet time. Ethiopian Jews, Haredi (Ultra-Orthodox people who often reject modern secular culture) and many Muslims, as well as a lot of Israeli teens, gathered for the Purim concert.

Heatherly's team was asked why the roses, and they responded to the people saying that they support Israel and love her people and wanted to say they stand with them because God loves them. It was such a sweet time, unlike the night before. The people were touched that they would show love to Israel. Randy was asked about the roses by an Orthodox man. He shared about the love of God. He was able to share his story and the Gospel, the word of his testimony. While there were no prayers, there was a deep time of listening and hearing each other.

Our group chose to go to the Jewish Quarter, knowing we might have a more difficult time than the rest. Daniel encouraged us to walk into the gate and the official area of the Jewish Quarter. I found a cool archway in which to sit with the keyboard and roses. Dave, Yara,

Khalida and Sheilah all ventured further in as I stayed back with Bibi and Daniel flanking me on either side. It was a perfect spot to sing. As people walked by, Bibi and Daniel offered roses and most people were receptive. A few would read the card and give back the rose, but they were gentle about it. Dave and the rest of the team returned for more roses in about a half hour or so. We only had a bucket left. Daniel suggested we move the keyboard again—further into the Jewish quarter.

Just as I pulled up my keyboard and got ready to change locations, an older Jewish man, clearly Orthodox, started talking at us, saying we should leave and go to the Christian Quarter and stay away from the Jewish people. He was angry and said he would call the police if we didn't leave, then walked away. Daniel felt he was bluffing and suggested we just stay where we were. So, I sat down again and began singing as the whole team spread out around me giving everyone roses. People were still celebrating Purim so there were many costumes, most of them lighthearted or beautiful. But within 15 to 20 minutes, with half a bucket to go, the old man returned and began screaming that we were missionaries, and he literally yanked the roses out of the hands of Jewish people who had received them. Snapping them in two he yelled at us to get out.

Every Jewish person within earshot or eyesight of the old man was told we were missionaries and they shouldn't accept a rose from us, or he physically ripped the rose away from some people, not allowing them to make their own choices. Daniel said we needed to go because he was creating a scene. The old man disappeared after we cleared out of the Jewish Quarter, but a younger man with a video camera and his buddy showed up suddenly and followed us quite a ways, laughing and saying all kinds of things in English and Hebrew to incite us. Our team remained fairly calm as we walked. Bibi tried to engage a couple of times but he didn't want a real conversation. As we approached where the van was parked, Daniel told us to wait for them to leave. Daniel finally walked over to the van while the two men were distracted by Khalida and Sheilah. They continued to hang around, so

Daniel drove by without stopping (to make sure the men harassing us didn't photograph the license plate to identify Daniel and his mission). I tried to flag some cabbies down, but we were already part way down Mt. Zion and all the cabs were full. So Yara, Khalida, and Sheilah went back up the hill to get a cab. They eventually found a van-cab driven by an Arab who picked us up and took us back to the hotel. The driver knew the guy who was filming us and said he had watched many of his films. He said the guy did it to everyone who wasn't Jewish and the police were pretty sick of him already.

3/26/2016

None of the Messianic congregations had opened their doors to our group to allow us to share or give out roses. But Sam was familiar with the congregation meeting at Christ Church, so he went to speak with the pastor. Even though it was last minute, they let the team give roses to the congregation while I sang a song. Afterward, one of their leadership said how much they appreciated the humble approach we took. No one had ever come and done something just to bless them. The whole congregation was very touched.

Later that day, Khalida and Sheilah ended up ministering to a Muslim shopkeeper in the shuk. He asked them what does it mean to be a Christian. He was confused by all the denominations. But he had been reading about Christianity and had seen our team giving out roses. He had been really touched by Jews and Arabs being here in the same space; living, eating, and working together. He asked how God could have a son. His friend came in and started saying our group worshipped many gods. He kicked his friend out of his store, saying: "I don't want to hear you, I want to hear them!" He asked Khalida and Sheilah to pray for him to have understanding.

Sheilah also shared later how they were shopping in the Shuk and the Lord told them to go into a particular store. Khalida spoke with the Muslim shopkeeper and after about 20 minutes she was praying with him. He said our group is very well-known in the Shuk. He told us the shopkeepers see our love and joy and are very interested in what we have. This is an answer to prayer.

3/27/2016

Today we worshiped at the Garden Tomb in Jerusalem as dawn slowly broke over the city. There were 1,500 people singing praises to God in the yawning hours of the morning. We gave out the last of our roses as people exited down the lane after the service. Later, we visited the Jerusalem Alliance Church lead by Pastor Mazen. We had an amazing time of worship in this little Arabic church tucked away in one of the many little side-streets of the Old City. After lunch Randy, Mazzen, Dave, and Yara walked the many steps over to the Western Wall. It is the last standing wall of the Jewish Temple that was destroyed in 70 AD, as Jesus said it would be. It has also been a place of God's visitation in my life each of the five times I have visited Jerusalem. It happened that our arrival at the Wall coincided with a beautiful bride preparing for her wedding, all in white, davening and praying there. It struck me as very symbolic of Messiah's bride, who, even through all her trials and tribulations worldwide, is being made ready for that special day when she will present herself spotless, without blemish before the Holy One. I touched the cold ancient stone and let my heart call out to God and listened. It was good. He is risen. He is risen indeed!

During the planning of this project I felt strongly that the team should not engage in any kind of political discussion or debate. Our focus needed to rest solely upon Jesus. At one point we were sharing a meal together and a friend, on mission with a well-known organization in Jerusalem, sat at table with us and began talking about the current political scene. About five minutes into the budding discussion, I explained about our rule for this trip. We would not engage in any kind of political talk, whether on the street, with friends, or in our rooms. Our focus needed to be, as much as possible, on Jesus. She seemed a bit put off when I initially explained, but she graciously accepted what I was saying and didn't continue that particular conversation.

It was not an easy thing to do—to confront her in this way. I tried to be gentle, but had no idea how she received it until the end of our stay in Jerusalem. At the Arabic church for the mid-morning Easter service, she came to meet us there. Sitting down beside me, she thanked me for what I had said to her about politics. She explained how when she first came to work with the ministry in Jerusalem, she was excited about the opportunity to grow closer to God. But that was not her experience. Instead, she encountered people who seemed more excited about politics than about the Lord. Over time she drifted in that direction. She thanked me for reminding her of what she had originally hoped to pursue in Israel while serving with this ministry—a deeper walk with Jesus.

I was thankful she came and told me. Most of the time we don't know the effect of the seeds sown during a project like this, but every now and then we get a glimpse.

For all of us on this particular team, this project was life-changing. Each one of us came to it with some level of fear or concern—yet all of us felt God had truly called us to minister His loving-kindness to Israeli and Arab alike—and especially to the Palestinians. What often boggles my mind is how God speaks to us and deals with our own hearts even as we become instruments of His grace.

I asked each of the team members to share their overall perspectives about this particular project. Below are a few of their take-away moments.

"I am so grateful for the whole team. For our unity and love, for standing, praying, and encouraging one another in spite of different difficulties and spiritual warfare.

The Lord was working in my heart during this mission and gave me deeper revelation, understanding, and love for Jews and Arabs. He took away my fear of Muslims. Now I can pray with more passion for them and look at them with love and smile.

During one Friday, we went to the Jewish Orthodox part of Jerusalem, where we faced strong opposition and rejection. It wasn't an easy experience but it was a very important lesson and it gave me the opportunity to see and understand more than before. This event gave me more compassion and desire to pray for Orthodox Jews and ask the Lord to remove the veil from their eyes and hearts. May God's love touch and set them free!"

(Brygida "Bibi" Rusek)

"What stood out for me the most is how open the heart of the Arab Palestinian is to love. As I was talking to many of them, they first started asking why we were there. After we gave them roses, they told me they have never been loved that way. Their hearts were touched and changed because they could see and feel the love of God through us. It was amazing to see the change on their faces, the smiles and the soft hearts. When we were in Bethlehem and I was talking to three young ladies that were getting ready to pray to receive the Lord, one of them said to me, 'I see a light in you. I want to kiss your face.' And she did. I trust that in that moment she had seen the light of the Lord in me. That was amazing to be the light in the darkness. As a team, we were God's hands and feet to hurting and broken hearts. We brought love to people who had never been loved. The glory and honor belong to our God and King."

(Khalida Wukawitz)

"Very soon into the trip, I needed to repent of buying into the fear the media has instilled in my heart that Muslims, particularly Muslim women who stood out because of some level of head covering, hated me and didn't want anything to do with me. I also had fears that had been instilled in me due to the terrorism... As I started interacting with people, both men and women, I saw the hunger in their eyes as they would talk about their dreams of peace. I was especially touched by the many young women I talked with who were so touched that we would bring them a rose and just love them, both Palestinian and Jewish. All fear of rejection and hate broke off my heart."

(Karen Wevick)

"The first time we met Pavo, a Catholic priest, he had the biggest smile on his face. I remember thinking that the joy of the Lord shone from his face. He had just finished leading his group in a time of worship in the chapel in the Holy Land Hotel in Bethlehem. I believe there were four from our group who went to the chapel to check on the roses, which were stored and worked on in the chapel. Pavo spoke very limited English so we struggled to outline a strategy for working on the roses that would not interfere with the worship time of his group. As we were trying to communicate, one person in our group busted out singing 'Nothing But The Blood of Jesus.' That big smile of joy I saw on Pavo's face at first returned as he sang along. When we finished singing, we all laughed and I didn't know it yet, but the Lord was showing us that despite our differences, we are united through His blood. And when we are unified in love, He is what people see.

Pavo invited our group to join his group from Croatia the next night for worship and we agreed. It was a sweet time of worship in unity and love. We spoke different languages, we came from different cultures, and there were even some theological differences between us, but with our eyes on worshiping the one and only true God, none of it mattered. We clapped as they sang in Croatian and they clapped as we sang in English. Part way into our worship time together we realized some of the group from Croatia spoke German.

Jurgen also spoke German, so we began a conversation, English to German, German to German, German to Croatian and back in reverse order. The first question Pavo asked was 'Why are you here?' Sally began her answer with the scripture the Lord put on her heart, John 17. As soon as Pavo heard John 17 he clapped his hands and said 'Holy Spirit, Holy Spirit.' Many in his group had amazed looks on their faces. John 17 was also the scripture the Lord was speaking to them. We shared many things between us that night, including healing that the Lord was doing in our hearts. It was beautiful.

Over the next few days, every time we saw our Croatian brothers and sisters we would 'greet one another with a holy kiss' and the love of the Lord. This love between people who were strangers to one another before meeting at the hotel did not go unnoticed by the Muslim staff. Before our three days at the hotel were up, two of the Muslim staff asked to receive Yeshua as Lord and Savior."

(Sheilah Dabb)

19

FOR SUCH A TIME AS THIS

"For we are His workmanship, created in Christ Jesus for good works, which God prepared beforehand that we should walk in them."

(Ephesians 2:10 NKJV)

"And who knows but that you have come to royal position for such a time as this?"

(Esther 4:14)

We celebrated the end of the 2016 project in Jerusalem and Bethlehem by spending a day debriefing. We shared our thoughts and feelings about the project while touring some of the Land. Out on the Sea of Galilee the team worshiped, prayed, and reflected on all that had transpired. I sat at the very back of the boat, crying. It was an amazing trip, but also hard. Call it tension release or something deeper, but I distinctly remember saying in my heart to God, *OK, we did it! Thanks! Done now.*

And I received the soft but firm, unmistakable response, *You'll be back.*

And so it was that in 2017 I found myself preparing yet another special *A Tour of Roses* project with its focus solely on the Palestinians. I felt the Lord reveal Hannukah—the Feast of Rededication—as the time period for this next endeavor. Hannukah usually occurs in December sometime on-or-before Christmas.

Looking back on the first project in Israel, I realize the Lord originally spoke to me about reaching out to the Palestinians, not the Israelis. But as I prayed and processed and eventually prepared, I had trouble accepting that. I kept pleading my case to include the Israelis as well as the Palestinians. Surely that was Scriptural—"to the Jew first." But I never received anything further in that direction.

God is gracious. And I am grateful for His incredible faithfulness and ability to redeem even our mistakes. I have had to come to terms with the fact that I didn't purely follow through on what He originally placed in my heart as His vision, but insisted on some of my own agenda. I can't help but wonder if that was the reason for some of the problems we encountered in Jerusalem as we tried reaching out to the Jewish population, and if it also occasioned the need to return to Bethlehem.

Having successfully led a team of sixteen other people on the previous project, I anticipated a similarly sized team for the December 2017 *ATOR*, especially since we were planning women's conferences in Bethlehem and Jericho.

Many people initially expressed interest, but as weeks wore on, only a few came forward to actually apply or commit. About a month before the application deadline in October, I was praying with my dear friend, Mary, and she felt clearly from the Lord the team would be small—about 4-5 people at most. I had not yet given up on the idea of a larger team. A lot of people had shown interest and were still thinking it over and praying. When Mary gave me that word, it was most certainly not what I wanted to hear, but it was exactly what God did. In the end, there were four of us, plus Danny from Holy Land Missions, who had participated in the previous project.

Another unusual pre-tour revelation occurred less than a week before departure. I was idly cruising my email account, noticing some of the news headlines. I came across a little article stating President

Trump was expected to make a special announcement on Monday December 4th, possibly revealing the US Embassy in Israel would be transferred from Tel Aviv to Jerusalem—thereby acknowledging Jerusalem as the true capital of Israel.

I'm not the one who usually keeps tabs on the news. Michael often informs me about things he thinks need to be known. That said, on this particular occasion I happened upon this piece myself—or maybe it found me.

My husband scanned all the media on Monday, December 4th, but couldn't find one word about the President's decision. Reasonably certain nothing more had transpired regarding the embassy in Israel, we boarded the plane as planned early Tuesday morning, December 5th, on our way to Tel Aviv. We landed at Ben Gurion International Wednesday morning, December 6th, amid the immediate aftermath of President Trump's decision to move the embassy to Jerusalem. It quickly became apparent God had sovereignly brought us there "for such a time as this."

The very next day Michael sent out a special missive to everyone receiving the prayer letter:

Dear Friends of ATOR,

I am sending this short update out this morning to address and hopefully allay concerns you may have regarding our ATOR Team Members currently on a mission from God in the Heart of the Holy Land, Bethlehem... EVERYONE IS OK. You are currently reading in your news sources that today has been labeled "A Day of Rage" in Israel by the forces upset with President Trump's announcement the United States will henceforth recognize Jerusalem as the capital of Israel.

As I mentioned yesterday we, at ATOR, do everything we can to steer clear of politics when abroad on a mission. But sometimes the political finds us whether we want it to or not.

I will not comment on the situation over there except to say it is extremely inconvenient toward our plans and itinerary to have this happening in Israel right now. But we also believe God knew exactly what He was doing when He called this team "for such a time as this" to minister to the very people who are raging in the streets and media this very day.

That said, here is what I know. Sent directly from Sally a few hours ago:

"Please keep all of the A Tour of Roses team in prayer as we are currently in Bethlehem very near one of the main checkpoints and the situation is very tense and angry right now. The checkpoint is closed and Bethlehem is on a 3-day strike with shops closed, etc.

We were blessed to be able to give our roses in Manger Square and worship the Lord only a few hours after demonstrations took place there also. God sent us here at this time to be an expression of His love in this moment.

Pray we are continually filled with the Lord's Spirit and His love trusting entirely in Him and that He would lead us wherever He wants us to go. Please pray also for the many Palestinians who are being deprived of their livelihood and provision because of the current situation. It is only because of your prayers that we have strength and grace and wisdom. Thank you for supporting us in prayer and encouragement!"

Sally did mention privately to me that there was tear gas in the streets. This is confirmed by an account I read in the L.A. Times:

"Clashes flared between the protesters and Israeli troops, who deployed water cannons and fired what appeared to be rubber bullets and tear gas to disperse the demonstrators."

—Michael

We decided to take roses first to a convalescent home. Georgette, one of the Palestinian women helping us, knew this place fairly well. Afterward we would see about possibly going to Manger Square a few hours later.

All the shops in and around Manger Square were closed and we weren't sure where to park. But we had extreme favor because one of the Palestinians who came with us knew the man handling the Nativity Church Parking. He let us in. The man in charge of the parking felt it was especially dangerous for me to sing. He thought the roses might be ok, but not my singing. After all, it had only been two or three hours since they demonstrated there, burning the American flag and a picture of President Trump. Sobered by what he said, I put the keyboard back. We prayed and I realized we needed to walk the area and pray.

Some Palestinian kids were selling hot buttered cups of corn kernels. We bought a few of those to warm up, and just continued pacing off the Square in prayer. As we did, Danny ran into a very good friend of his, a Muslim taxi-driver. He arranged police covering and security for us. At that point the police were willing to keep an eye on us so we all agreed to give it a try. Taking the keyboard and about 300 roses back out, we made our way to The Bethlehem Peace Center and for almost an hour we worshiped and gave out roses.

On our way back to the hotel it got a little scary. About a block away from the hotel, another group of demonstrators crowded the checkpoint. We hurried out of the van to the sliding glass lobby doors of the hotel but they were locked. We banged, rang, knocked and eventually they opened up as the tear gas started again. It smelled awful. But I learned a fascinating fact. Lemon Honey mentholated cough drops seem to dilute the effects from the tear gas. Danny, who was in agony because of the effect on his sinuses, discovered the cough drops absolutely quelled all his symptoms, and he had no further issues with his sinuses.

The next day there were many angry messages broadcast from mosques over the loudspeakers in different parts of Bethlehem and elsewhere because it was a Muslim holy day. But even as those messages went out all over the city, so did roses in pockets of Beit Sahour and Bethlehem, sowing God's love and peace in the hearts of those who were able to welcome it. And many received with joy and thankfulness. For such a time as this!

I prayed with the pharmacist across the street. She was a believer, but felt afraid and was grateful for prayer. The Lord gave me extra boldness as I walked into a store with about six very hard looking men and gave five of them roses. There were no women in the store at all. The men were all surprisingly receptive, except the last man who wouldn't accept a rose but kept staring at me.

That evening Danny and I met Mohammed as we were giving roses out on the streets and in the shops of Beit Sahour. When we entered his shop he was incredibly hospitable. He read the rose card and asked why we were doing it there and not in Jerusalem. I explained I am Jewish and felt God put it on my heart to bring roses for the Palestinians right now. Mohammed was so moved that he asked Danny and I to wait a few minutes while he left us in charge and ran down the street. We were a little nervous because he didn't come back right away. But when he returned he had a cold liter of Coke in one hand and a couple chocolate bars in the other. He poured the Coke into cups and we shared the chocolate together. It was a very beautiful moment.

The following morning we were all up extra early, preparing for the conference. Because of the perilous situation, none of us knew if any of the women who signed up would actually show up. Amazingly, about 60-70 women braved their way through blockades and rioting, etc. to participate in our little *Something Beautiful for Someone Beautiful Conference*. With demonstrations and tear gas happening only blocks away, Marlys, Sharon, and I shared our testimonies with both young and old Palestinian women who spent most of the day with us. We began by praying individually for every woman who attended that morning in preparation for the conference. And there were even some ladies willing to let us wash their feet. During the actual conference we shared about loving God, loving ourselves, and loving others.

It was a profound time considering all that was going on outside those walls. Marlys and I anointed and prayed for each woman who came. Sharon and Bibi washed the feet and prayed over the 4-5 women who were willing to try this new experience.

It was one of the most intimate moments of the day for me. I looked into their faces and put my hand on their shoulders and prayed as I felt God leading. Afterward, many of their faces seemed lighter and they thanked me.

Another powerful moment occurred right at the beginning of the actual program. Marlys, who turned 79 during the project, shared how she remained in an abusive marriage for 41 years. When she finally found the courage to divorce her husband, even though she still loved him, he shot her through the heart at point blank range.

Many of the women cried. Most couldn't believe something like that happened in America. After the project, Marlys reflected: "I was first to speak. The response was amazing! They asked questions afterward and couldn't believe I had stayed in such an abusive situation for so many years, especially living in America. The last woman who was allowed to ask a question actually told me, 'You are like Jesus. You were persecuted and provoked—and killed.' And it was like I kind of fell apart. I just started sobbing—to have someone tell me that—because I thought to myself—no, I am not like Jesus, it's just me—Marlys. The translator came over afterward to hug me. And I sobbed in her arms."

Later, others were deeply impacted by the issue of forgiveness through what Sharon and I shared. The conference ended with each woman taking a rose to give to the person God put on their hearts as a way of expressing love and forgiveness.

During one of the prayer times that day, Bibi prayed for one mother whose son was killed by Muslims because he was a Christian and refused to become Muslim. Bibi shared with her about the difference between forgiving and forgetting, and that forgiveness is a decision not an emotion.

The woman agreed and said, "I forgave him, but I still have anger." Bibi told her we can ask for the Lord's help and said she would pray for her, but also encouraged the woman to pray for herself and give her anger to the Lord. Bibi interceded and afterward the woman also prayed, giving the Lord her anger.

That Sunday we ventured out again to Manger Square and Danny was able to reunite with a Palestinian police officer he had met in July of 2016. Danny was glad to see him and the officer provided VIP parking for our van. Again, I brought my keyboard and began worshiping as the rest of the team gave out roses to vendors and people wandering through the Square. There were many different reactions.

Bibi took some roses to a few young women who were very happy to receive them. But a young man with his friends came and he was angry and upset. He told the women not to receive the roses because there was Hebrew writing on the cards also. He said Israel is his enemy and we should write on the cards only in Arabic. So Bibi tried to explain to him that God loves Palestinians and Israelis, but he wasn't open to another point of view. He started talking about President Trump and asked Bibi how she felt about President Trump. He asked if she agreed with the decision of President Trump. Bibi didn't want to share her opinion and so diplomatically ended the conversation.

Marlys encountered some more gentlemen who were very angry about President Trump and what he had done. They asked, "Where are you from?"

"I am from America"

They gave back the rose and said, "I don't want it."

Sometimes that was all they did, and then there were others who wanted to talk with her about it. Marlys explained, "We are not here for anything political."

"Do you agree with President Trump?"

She responded, "We are just here to show God's love for you."

And sometimes they would keep the rose once she explained everything but other times the person would give it back. She would still bless them. A couple times when they walked away without a rose they would tell her, "God bless you too!"

One man said, "Why do you have Hebrew on this card?"

And she didn't know what to say, but the Holy Spirit knew what to say. Marlys responded, "Because we want everyone to read the card so that everyone can love each other."

Once Marlys explained it to him in that way he said, "Oh, yeah, we should all love one another." And he was really happy and walked away with a rose in his hand.

Later that day we drove into Jericho at sunset. Having never visited Jericho previous to this project I had no idea how much risk was involved in staying there, especially during this particularly volatile time. No formal checkpoint existed except some warning signs at the town line. There were several noticeable burns in the pavement and discarded tires alongside. The road was pockmarked and rough as we entered. Thankfully, our accommodations were all the way over on the far side of the main commercial area.

As we arrived at the hotel, the surroundings seemed completely disassociated from what we saw driving through town. But when we emerged from the van, we heard a loud sound of cheering and yelling. Danny, in his effort to assuage our fears, said it was probably a soccer match. But in the early morning hours the next day I could still hear the shouting. I realized people were still publicly reacting to the embassy being moved, and our presence in town might not be welcome. We had planned to bring the women's conference we offered in Bethlehem to the believers in Jericho, but that idea soon evaporated in the wake of the day's events.

After preparing some of the roses during the morning and handing out many to the hotel staff, we carefully, prayerfully decided to have lunch in the town center first, at a little sandwich shop where Danny knew the owner. From there we agreed to walk and pray through the main square. Everything went well. We even met up with police and talked with them about what we intended to do, and after some consideration they permitted us to give out the roses.

People loved the roses! We must have given out at least 300. It was as if they were starved for something beautiful and the kindness the roses signified. For the most part, everyone was very positive about the American people. As word got out, traffic stopped up a bit around us as people received roses in their cars. Good words and smiles were exchanged.

Our buckets were empty in under a half hour so we got back into the van to drive to the hotel. We hadn't told anyone where we were going, but an unmarked car followed us. At some point Danny pulled the van over to see if the car behind was intentionally following us, and they pulled over also.

There were two men in the car. One man got out and approached Danny on the driver's side. He identified himself as some kind of officer with the police department. He was extremely hostile and angry beyond measure, especially toward Americans. Honestly, he was very frightening and appeared to be enraged in a way that seemed spiritually infused. I explained that we had come very specifically to give out roses as a way of sharing the love of God, even in this difficult time. But the officer responded by saying that roses were like bombs. He wanted to know where we were staying but Daniel felt it was probably dangerous to tell these men anything specific. They wanted us to leave Jericho and Daniel felt we should drive out of Jericho to the Dead Sea, which was only a few kilometers away. But we couldn't get out of the city because the people had already started demonstrating and rioting again. So, we made a U-turn but the police car continued following us. Danny suggested we stop at a large sycamore tree, which was a historical landmark, and take pictures to buy ourselves a little time.

There was an old street vendor by the tree who loved our *ATOR* shirts. I purchased a couple of items for a higher price than needed and so did Marlys, to buy some time in the hope the situation would cool down. We talked with the street vendor also. He was very kind and helped me de-stress a little. The police officer finally emerged from his car, when he saw we weren't leaving right away, and started talking to Danny and me.

He reiterated how much he hated Americans and President Trump and how Jerusalem belongs to Palestine. I showed him the back of the t-shirt and said, "We aren't here for President Trump. We are here for God. Only God. We brought the roses to show love to your people."

After a little while, he started calming down. He even smiled a couple times. When he found out Bibi was Polish he got excited, exclaiming how much he loved Poland. He wanted to know where we were going and Danny said we were heading to the Dead Sea but the way was blocked. He said he knew a different way and would lead us out. I thanked the vendor. He really liked my t-shirt a lot so I took it off and gave it to him. Fortunately, I was wearing another shirt underneath.

The officer led us out of Jericho and pointed to the Dead Sea, admonishing us that it wasn't safe to remain in Jericho. We didn't know what to do or where to go next. We were worried we wouldn't get a refund from the hotel. Of even greater concern was whether or not it was even safe for us to return to the hotel that night—given the officer's warning—and pack up the remaining roses and our things.

Danny wanted to return to Bethlehem. I felt we had already done what we needed to do there and maybe we should head for Jerusalem after all. It would also probably be safer. But as we talked, Danny reminded me how much more expensive staying in Jerusalem would be. At that point I suggested we pray.

As soon as I said "Amen" and opened my eyes, I looked at Bibi. Immediately I remembered The Father's House on the Mt. of Olives, a place Bibi visits several times a year to intercede in Jerusalem. It is a house of prayer that also offers limited accommodations. The Father's House was planted by a German church in Berlin, where I had shared in concert as part of a previous *ATOR* project in 2013. It certainly seemed this might be God's provision. Bibi had been thinking the very same thing but was waiting for God's confirmation.

The Father's House turned out to be entirely God's grace to us in every way. It is a peace-filled community of prayer in an extremely conflicted area. The Jericho resort gave us a generous refund for the meals and days we couldn't stay. They were gracious to us in every way and very understanding. We left a generous tip, as we also did in Bethlehem.

There was no way we would have been able to fit all the roses, luggage, and ourselves into one van. Thankfully, God again provided. A friend of Bibi's was kind enough to drive out from Jerusalem to Jericho and take most of the team in his car, along with some luggage and other items. Thanks to his extra vehicle, our luggage, team members, and all 1,500 roses made it out in one trip.

The following day we gave out roses in the Shuk. I brought my keyboard and worshiped. I was still processing all that happened in Jericho, wondering if I had made a mistake trying to minister under the current conditions. But during our outreach at the Shuk, we met Ibrahim who lives in Jericho and works in Jerusalem. He recognized Danny and me from our time in the town square in Jericho. He said he liked what we were doing. That was so encouraging to hear. I felt in that moment that if even one person in Jericho understood or was touched, then it wasn't in vain.

Danny gave roses to two young Israelis, and began talking with them as they asked what the purpose of this project was. Danny shared about the love of Yeshua for all mankind, especially His people— Israel: "They were a bit taken aback by the way I pronounced the Lord's name. I gave a brief history of who I was before Jesus and how through Him not only do I have everlasting life, but I look at people in a new way. I am thankful for His healing in my life. They listened and said that they thought it was a beautiful way of showing God's love. I encouraged them saying, 'Things will get tough in Jerusalem but all you need is Yeshua.' Before they left I invited them to make an honest investigation of the person of Jesus. One of them said he would."

There was also a Jewish woman who hugged Danny and blessed me so much in her expression, as she spoke the words, "*Ha Kavod*" which means, the glory of God. It was obvious she really understood the heart of what we were doing. There were many people who saw the beauty and significance of what we had been sharing in the past few days and it touched them deeply.

Bibi made sure to give roses to Johnny (who helped drive us out of Jericho) and his brother who has a shop in the Shuk. Thinking about how to bless them in return for all they did for us, Bibi wondered if she should give them roses again. She and another team member were close to his shop in the Shuk and the men saw them from a distance and shouted, "Girls, cake is waiting for you!" So they went to the shop and saw another man who was their friend and had not received a rose yet. So they gave him a rose, Johnny and his brother also. And they told Bibi, "We are going to visit a Muslim family and we will give them these roses."

He also mentioned that when he was visiting the Muslim family he had prayed for their son who had a tumor. A few days later when he returned the tumor was gone. No bleeding and no other sign of this tumor. And he said today, "I asked Johnny to come with me because I don't speak Arabic. So we will go there together to share about the Lord with them. And these roses are like a great blessing. We would like to give them to this family."

That Friday we took the roses to East Jerusalem, which was considered very volatile. But as it turned out, the people on the streets, shopkeepers, and even bus drivers were very receptive to the roses.

The first place we stopped we gave out roses on either side of the street. Overall, people received them with great appreciation. There were some men standing together in one of the business areas. One man was obviously Orthodox Jewish and the others were Palestinian. The Jewish man received the rose and gave it to his Palestinian friend, the man who owned the business. And they told me how they are brothers and friends together and they each had an arm around the other—it was really beautiful!

When we drove to our second stop, it was much closer to Damascus Gate—but on the other side of the street. Many people received from us gladly. But we made a choice toward the end to give some of our roses inside the Israeli police station. Some people saw us go in with the roses. There was only one officer on duty—a young man. He was very appreciative of receiving the rose and said there was another officer at the station, but he was getting lunch. We left an extra rose for him.

After exiting the police station we gave out some more roses and I encountered three beautiful young Muslim women and handed them each a rose. They were clearly delighted and asked where we were from as they read the card. They wanted to take a selfie with me and their roses, but a man from across the street started yelling to them in Arabic. He sounded very angry.

The one girl who spoke English fairly well asked if I was with the Israelis. I said, "I am from America."

She asked, "Why is there Hebrew on the card also?"

And I said, "We want everyone to read it and to learn how to love each other."

The man was still yelling at intervals as she and I were talking. I asked her to tell me what he was saying but she wouldn't. So I said, "I don't see labels. I see people, and God loves people."

She finally said, "I don't think so," and handed her rose back to me, as did her two friends. Then they walked away.

That night we gathered for a Shabbat dinner at The Father's House with believers from Germany and New Zealand. For Sharon, it was the highlight of her day. Sharon especially enjoyed the worship and shared: "We had a time of spontaneous worship in three different languages with various instruments. That was so awesome! I really got a sense of what Heaven will be like."

I made my mom's version of Matzo Ball Chicken soup, which everyone loved. As the evening began I quickly became aware of the German guests who joined us for dinner. One woman, apparently a leader in the community, knew all the blessings for Shabbat and Hannukah, and in Hebrew no less. She was more than proficient. She was impassioned. And yet I, the token Jew at the table, could only recite the basic prayers over the bread and wine. She seemed to know more of my culture than I did, which again stirred up my struggle with my identity as a Jew who believes in Jesus. I have to admit I felt inadequate in that moment and wanted to withdraw. But God had other plans.

Later in the evening the conversation rolled around to why we were in Jerusalem at this time and what exactly was *A Tour of Roses*. The Germans seemed particularly interested. The leader translated as I shared the story with the three of them how *A Tour of Roses* began. Once again, I witnessed the power of love and forgiveness as the Germans were in tears by the end of my story. I knew it was a divine appointment.

Our final outreach was at Damascus Gate. We only had a bucket or so of roses left, but we all felt strongly to bring them to this especially difficult location. As we approached with the van, the area was packed out with crowds of people and the IDF were everywhere. Bibi suggested I ask the soldiers for permission to hand out roses and sing with my keyboard. I was not inclined to risk hearing a "no" from them and having to regroup. I had little faith they would respond otherwise. But Bibi was quietly persistent in her way and sure enough, I wound up asking them for permission. Much to my amazement, they pointed at a particular spot where they would permit me to sit with my keyboard and play until they said otherwise. I did just that.

I was amazed by the response of people to the music even before the roses arrived. God drew people to us and the team casually spoke with several different people while I continued to worship, including some of the press who were lined up in rows by the time we left. One young Australian man walked directly up toward us to encourage me by saying: "This is exactly what is needed. You are changing the atmosphere as you worship. Hallelujah!"

I had started singing right away, but Danny had to park and then bring the last bucket of roses to where we were. In the meantime, there were a lot of people who just stood and listened. Marlys saw one man go behind me and read the back of my shirt.

Everybody was pleased to get a rose and read the card. Several people just stopped and listened to the music after they received the rose and read the card. When we finished giving out all the roses there were still people coming up wanting roses. Sharon had some cards from the roses in her purse—so she was handing those out.

Toward the end, just before the police told us that we had to leave because there was going to be a demonstration shortly, there was one young lady that was asking questions. Sharon gave her a card and she was very interested in what we were doing and where we came from. So Marlys and Sharon both answered her—back and forth—saying that we were there to show God's love for her and all of the people there. She still kept asking questions. Then she started asking about political stuff. They continued to respond by saying we weren't there for anything political. We only came to express God's love. She was just grateful to hear everything they had to say. Then her husband walked up and told her they had to go. But she stayed and continued talking with Marlys and Sharon, who just kept saying we are here to show God loves you and nothing political. She relayed that to her husband, but I don't think he really got it. He just wanted her to leave. In the end she had to go with him and that's when several police came down and said for our own safety we had to leave.

During our time in Damascus Square, Bibi also had some encounters. She was giving out roses to people who were walking up the stairs and some of them were asking questions. She spoke a little bit longer with a man from India. He was very interested and amazed. He said that we were doing something important and beautiful, especially in this place where so many fights have been taking place.

Even a few days before there had been a big fight and Israeli soldiers had to intervene.

Bibi also spoke with three people from Holland. They asked what we were doing. They were also very supportive and encouraging. They said, "May God bless you!"

When I was worshiping, Bibi noticed one Jewish man who was walking up the stairs but stopped and started listening. He was standing for a longer time and she could see he was very attentive. I was singing a song about Jesus right then and he started to leave. Bibi smiled at him and he smiled back. She was praying for him as he listened.

Danny told us later of his encounter with two young Palestinian men at Damascus Gate who were very curious about what we were doing. They didn't understand why we would travel all the way from America to talk about how Jesus came all the way from Heaven to demonstrate His love for all of us.

I have found it is absolutely essential that we finish well, cleaning up after ourselves in every possible way. To that end, we often pick up leaves, petals, cards, and other discards from our endeavors and dispose of them appropriately. This is an important part of respecting the people and land we are visiting.

In keeping with that protocol, we dropped off the extra towels, bowls, and miscellaneous goodies we didn't end up using in Jericho with Pastor Steve Khoury in Jerusalem, and then headed for the flower shop. Seven of our fifteen buckets were stolen and I was prepared to pay for them, but the owner wouldn't let me. I gave him a couple of our CDs and told him about our last wild adventure at Damascus Gate. I added that he had a part in it because of the beautiful roses he procured for us.

I saw him eyeing my *ATOR* hoodie and asked if he wanted it. At first he demurred, saying, "But it's your hoodie. You should keep it."

And I said, "If you really want it, I want you to have it."

He read the blessing on the back and for a long moment just looked at me. I handed him my hoodie and he said simply, "Thank you for coming"

SAR SHALOM
(Prince of Peace)

Between the dead and dying
Amid a war of words
The Prince of Peace is calling
One day He will be heard
By all the poor in spirit
The blind who long to see
Those who live in darkness
Everyone who will believe

CHORUS
Yeshua HaMashiach *
Adon HaKavod **
Desire of the nations
Promised One of old
Moshiach HaOlam ***
(He was) pierced for our transgressions
His blood bought release
He became our peace
Sar Shalom
Sar Shalom

In the ruin and ashes
Of dreams left unfulfilled
The voice of God is sounding
Stirring all who will rebuild
In long forgotten places
In willing wounded souls
There will be a planting
Of the Hope that makes us whole

CHORUS
(Bridge)
You walked through the walls
We raised up in our hurt and fear
Opened eyes and ears
So we could finally see and hear
The love that heals
The broken heart of man
CHORUS

EPILOGUE

I n this season of our ministry involving *A Tour of Roses*, it has first and foremost been about obedience. Not that I have always obeyed God perfectly. At any point I could have turned away from His leading and made a very good case for doing so. But by His grace I have not, and do not expect to. Each time the Lord has led me out of my comfort-zone to follow *His* leading, not mine, there has been healing in and through me—and in many of those who have come alongside in prayer and on the actual team.

"If you love me, keep my commands." (John 14:15)

"Jesus replied, Anyone who loves me will obey my teaching." (John 14:23)

Our love for God should drive our obedience. When we follow Him through our fears, doubts, and uncertainties we break through those barriers and taste a deeper, fuller experience of the freedom and joy God intends for us all.

I remember sitting in prayer on the Sunday after the violent shooting took place at a 2015 Christmas party in San Bernardino. I was overwhelmed by the thought of the survivors and how no Christmas party would ever seem the same to them. There would always be this traumatic memory.

As I pondered and prayed with our group I heard a holy whisper, *What about roses?* It was so impossible to my mind and sensibilities that roses could have any meaning at all for people so devastated by violence. I thought the last thing anyone would want were strangers coming into their personal space to offer them a red rose as they processed their grief and pain. But the idea wouldn't go away.

That week I challenged God to show me He was in this notion as I drove the hour or so out from my home to San Bernardino. Suffice it to say, He opened every door and poured out extreme favor. So much so, that when we actually showed up a week later with roses to give to the office workers, and all those surrounding them, the Lord provided escorts for my team in each of the buildings where workers were stationed. This was the day before President Obama was scheduled to visit. I remember Michael saying he wondered how we would even get into the buildings with all the Secret Service that had to be placed at each point. Not only did we get in, but we were accompanied by some of the employees, and the roses were received with tears and hugs and deep gratitude.

It was no different for the seventeen of us who ventured into Jerusalem and Bethlehem, during Purim week of 2016, to hand out 7,500 long stem red roses to Jews, Arabs, and Palestinians alike.

Not meaning to, we probably broke all kinds of rules and protocols. We worshiped in the Shuk (marketplace) in Jerusalem as my team fanned out into all the shops in the Arab Christian quarter and beyond, to offer wearied, cynical merchants the beauty and kindness of a red rose freely given because of Love. In Bethlehem we almost stopped traffic in front of our hotel the first time we gave out roses to all those driving and walking by. In Manger Square many were deeply moved through the love and worship expressed, and several Muslims prayed with us to ask Jesus into their hearts.

My new friend, Khalida, shared a moment that happened to her during the trip that is forever engraved in my memory. As soon as we entered Bethlehem it became very apparent that Khalida was the team evangelist. Born in Bethlehem, Khalida is partly Palestinian and speaks fluent Arabic. She has an amazing testimony of God's redemption in her life. At one point the Lord impressed on Khalida's heart she should especially offer her roses to the IDF soldiers (Israeli Defense Force) and tell them she is a Palestinian who loves them. This was something my other new friend, Mazzen, also Palestinian and born in Ramallah, chose to do as well.

Khalida approached one young soldier who was carrying his weapon across his chest, finger perpetually on or near the trigger. She presented him a rose, identifying herself as a Palestinian who loves Israel and the Jewish people. He suddenly turned to the side for a moment, which made Khalida pretty nervous and she prepared to walk away, not wishing to offend him or disrupt his work. But he quickly responded, saying he was putting his gun down so he could really talk with her. He didn't feel he could actually engage as long as the gun remained between them. He told Khalida that his wife refused to have children with him these last 3 or 4 years because she was afraid he would be stabbed, shot, or bombed by a Palestinian. He concluded by telling Khalida that tonight he would go home to his wife and tell her he met a Palestinian woman today who loves Israel and loves his people. And then they hugged.

How does the world change? One person at a time. I didn't set out expecting nations to be transformed because a few of us brought red roses into the streets and hearts of their people. And yet—who knows—perhaps God can use something as fragile and beautiful as a rose to speak the heart of His love to world-weary souls broken by pain and loss. I know one thing for sure, *I* have been changed, and many of those who have journeyed with me also have been changed. I certainly didn't plan it that way. But then—God.

In the end, it all belongs to the Maker and Creator of every living thing. He is the author of this idea and is well able to bring about His purposes and plans for every rose given, every seed planted, every hope sown. And in this I am mindful that His ways are not my ways. This is an ongoing revelation and lesson to me personally, and those who are walking this out alongside. And therefore, however it may appear, none of it is in vain when it belongs to Him.

ACKNOWLEDGMENTS

First and foremost I am thankful to Jesus who daily teaches me what it means to follow Him and learn to love as He has loved me. The truth is I stumble much more than I walk, but my Lord is gracious and patient with me beyond measure, for which I am very grateful.

I am thankful for my husband and collaborator-for-life, Michael O'Connor, who has many times offered me sage counsel to which I have sometimes listened, but who has always supported me in love and prayer. Without him *A Tour of Roses* could not have come into existence as it is.

I am thankful for our beautiful and amazing daughters, Dusty Rose (who helped edit this manuscript), Bonnie Joy, and Shannon Leigh. They have each paid a steep price for the ongoing journey Michael and I have elected to take in following Jesus onto the mission field. And they have each spoken into my life in profound ways by their choices in life.

I am also thankful for Pastor Paul and Kathy Bradshaw who have been pastors, mentors, and dear friends to me and my whole family. Your love, counsel, and ongoing obedience to God remain a continuing example of what it means to follow Jesus.

To our Board of Directors, past and present. Current board members: Paul Bradshaw, Steve Chesser, Gary Peyrot, Elaine Stover, Dawne Kotzen, and Dusty Rose Tsalkova. Michael and I thank you for standing and praying with us for the Lord's wisdom and direction, provision and protection, and grace in all things.

I am thankful for Ms. Deborah Darling (also a Jewish believer in Jesus) who faithfully followed the Lord to minister in Germany, and who shared with me one fateful day her concerns as she prepared to "set sail." Who knew one conversation would turn a lifetime of thinking on its head and ultimately give birth to *A Tour of Roses*.

I am grateful for my dear friend, Evi Hall—yet another Jewish believer—who, when I called out of the blue to invite her to explore God's invitation to Germany with me, eventually agreed. And what an adventure we had!

To my good friend, Avi Snyder of Jews for Jesus, who thankfully didn't think I was crazy, and was willing to help me dream a little way into *A Tour of Roses.*

To Karen Forth who helped me in innumerable ways in those early days of discovery, especially enabling me to talk with the residents of the tiny village of Brezinka, just outside the barbed wire of Auschwitz Birkenau, so I could better understand their side of the story.

To Magda Balcerak, my very dear Polish friend who challenged me to bring *ATOR* to Jedwabne, even after I had read the book, *Neighbors.* You loved me and helped me to see Poland through your eyes.

To Mark and Cathy Warwick, who gave up their comfortable lives in the UK and followed God's call to Poland. Thank you for coming along on the ride those first couple years with *ATOR.* You challenged me in so many ways that were needed.

To Wiola, for recounting her painfully honest exchange with the Lord, as she, along with Mark and Cathy, scouted out Jedwabne that first time.

To my very dear friend, Jurgen Schmutz, born in the community of Dachau, who continues to show me the beauty of what Germany can be through his ongoing humility, love, and kindness.

To Dagmar Menzel who toured me through the former concentration camp of Dachau the very first time in 2008, and stayed with me as we enjoyed dinner in town and then discovered that amazing English garden behind the castle walls.

To my good friend Rodney Stafford, who heard the Lord say I needed to come to Ireland, and then put his shoulder to the plow and learned how to schedule concerts for this "wandering Jew," so I might share our songs and stories with his people.

To my dear friend Donna Taggart, who welcomed me and our team to Northern Ireland so extravagantly. It is through your eyes I have seen some of Belfast, the Shankill Road, and the country you grew up in.

To Jack McKee, pastor of the amazing New Life Center that sits on the Peace Wall in Belfast. Thank you for allowing us to invade the church with roses and more roses, and all the beautiful insanity we got to share with some of the people like Julian and Andrew in your church, and many more on the Shankill and Falls Roads.

To Pastor Andreas Bauer of the German church in Berlin who warmly welcomed us there in 2013. Thank you for allowing us to find shelter on the Mt. of Olives with your prayer team as we were firmly escorted out from Jericho.

To Rabbi Michael Wolf who truly encouraged me and totally blessed me as one writer to another. I still remember how much it meant to me as I was in WA looking out over the river and crying over the phone as you shared your response to this book.

To my dear friend, Rabbi Chaim Urbach, who continually challenges me to understand better where I came from and who God has called me to be as a Jew who belongs to Messiah. Thank you for wrestling with me over the more difficult sections of this book.

To everyone who has prayed for Michael and I, and *A Tour of Roses* once or many times as we continue to walk out this strange and beautiful calling.

To everyone who has given in any way toward this project, enabling us to model the extravagant love of God through the tangible display of roses, and in every other way the Lord has led us.

To all my core team people on all the various trips: Hannah Lynn Musap, Marlys Nunneri, Diane Evert, Steven Skoglund, Magda Balcerak, Dagmar Menzel, Jurgen Schmutz, Elaine Stover, Sam and Heatherly Walker, Gayle Lenz, Brian O'Connor, Esther McCartney, Vincent Archer, Dave and Yara Panther, Sharon McMeans, Felicia Godinez, Rachel Jones, Joan Appleton McBride, Kathy Bradshaw, Marina Tafoya, Yvette Mora Leeper, Mary Makarios, Ken Shatto, Sally

Huggins, Lura Olander, Sunny Lehman, Amalia Lejbowicz, Del Leftwich, Brygida Rusek, Sharon Munoz Flores, Dusty Tsalkova, Bonnie O'Connor, Mallory Gish, Evi Hall, Beate Trinkner, Eric Weatherbee, Randy Dorn, Leonid Prouter, Marek and Kasia, Bozcena, Lauren Seitz, Alex Pistyur, Emily Fry, Karen Wevick, Khalida Wukawitz, Sheilah Dabb, Nic Sher, Mazzen Warra, Daniel Collins, Pamela Wrobel, Karen Forth, Mark and Cathy Warwick.

And to everyone not mentioned above—who has given out a rose with us in any capacity wherever we were—may the Lord continue to bless and encourage you to reach out with His extravagant love!

ABOUT THE AUTHOR

In 1990 Sally Klein O'Connor and her husband, Michael, began sharing their unique songs and stories across the United States through Improbable People Ministries.

In 2009 *A Tour of Roses* began as Sally led her first team giving out roses into the streets of Dachau, Bergen, and Oswiecim. *ATOR* has since visited many countries, including Northern Ireland, Israel, Hungary, Poland, Canada, and Belgium.

Sally and Michael reside in Southern California. They are the parents of three lovely daughters. Sally's first book, *Beauty in the Beast,* was originally published by Broadman and Holman in 2005.

If you would like more information about A Tour of Roses or the songs of Michael and Sally, you can find them at: atourofroses.com or improbablepeople.org

Write to Sally at Sally@songs4god.com

Made in the USA
Coppell, TX
26 October 2019